Strategic Management: A Resource

for the Hospitality and Tourism Industries

Richard Teare and Hadyn Ingram

Cassell
Wellington House
125 Strand
London WC2R 0BB

127 West 27th Street
New York
NY 10011

Copyright: Richard Teare and Hadyn Ingram 1993.

All rights reserved. No part of this publication may be reproduced or transmitted in any form or by any means, electronic or mechanical including photocopying, recording or any information or retrieval system, without prior permission in writing from the publishers.

First published 1993, Reprinted 1994, Reprinted 1996

British Library Cataloguing-in-Publication Data
A catalogue record for this book is available from the British Library.
ISBN 0 304 32867 7

Library of Congress Cataloging-in-Publication Data
A catalogue record for this book is available from the Library of Congress.

Typeset by Richard Teare
Printed and bound in Great Britain by Short Run Press Ltd., Exeter.

Current Titles in the Hospitality and Tourism Resource-Based Series:

Series Editor: Professor Richard Teare

- Strategic Management
- Marketing Management
- Operational Techniques
- Operations Management
- Management Skills

CASSELL

INTRODUCTION

OVERVIEW

Strategic management is traditionally viewed as the responsibility of senior management. Rocco Forte, chairman and chief executive of Forte PLC, thinks this is changing because market conditions are more unpredictable and competitors more numerous. He sees the need to stimulate a realignment of thinking and practice at the operational level so that unit managers perceive a wider dimension to their role.

Why a resource-based approach?
The concept of a resource-based approach to the study and practice of strategic management is centred on the need for a pragmatic, problem-solving orientation. Accordingly, the book draws from a number of existing publications in order to provide an affordable, easy-to-use guide to industry applications and examples. Industry relevance is assured by the use of detailed business cases to illustrate key principles.

Readership
A key consideration in the book's design and layout is flexibility of use. It is intended as a core text for courses at undergraduate and postgraduate level, as a resource for open/distance learning courses and short course programmes and as a convenient, easy-to-use reference guide for managers working at all organizational levels, and in both operational and specialized roles. To ensure continued relevance, the format of the book allows for regular updating and extension.

APPROACH

Introduction
Each chapter begins with an introductory overview of the topic, followed by a contents list and related reading references which can be found in the resource publications. Access to all of the listed publications is strongly recommended.

Review
The chapter review provides a summary of key issues, influences and changes relating to the topic area. Where appropriate, industry examples are used as illustrations and in some chapters, ideas originally developed and applied in manufacturing or other service industry settings are used to provide a wider perspective or to explain how hospitality/tourism firms might adapt existing practices.

Conclusion and extension
A concluding statement is followed by a series of review questions which relate to the key points raised in the chapter. In most cases, the review questions test comprehension of the topic material and relevant application by requiring the reader to draw from his or her industry observations and experience. All of the extension questions and exercises are linked to business case problems, opportunities and other scenarios.

Teaching and learning
It is my view that the resource-based approach is flexible enough to support and encourage a range of different teaching and learning activities. These include:

(a) Reader-centred, independent study and investigation, including some self-assessment using the review and extension material. In this situation the teacher facilitates the learning activity through tutorial discussion, workshop activity and group project work involving discussion, debate and presentations, among other interactive techniques.

(b) Resource material for open/distance learning courses whereby the reader works independently at his/her own pace to an agreed learning contract. The review and extension material is suitable for self-assessment and for seminar and syndicate work whenever course meetings take place.

(c) Specific focusing on business practices and strategic management applications in hospitality/tourism organizations, perhaps as part of a wider focus on the service industry sector.

(d) As a resource for the cross-fertilization of ideas and practices, especially in relation to the way in which the extension material is used.

Summarizing, the book can be used to facilitate independent learning, direct aspects of self-assessment and to support an array of individual and group project work, ranging from the updating and analysis of business trends and company information to interactive seminar and workshop activities.

I would like to thank Hadyn Ingram for his valued contribution to the resource-based series and the series publisher, Judith Entwisle-Baker.

Richard Teare
Series Editor

CONTENTS

Part 1: Strategic Planning

1. **Structures**
   Interrelationships between organizational design, characteristics, functions and strategic behaviour (flexibility, responsiveness, capability).

2. **Processes**
   Planning process functions with reference to managerial roles and styles, decision models, generic strategies and the formulation of strategy.

3. **Procedures**
   Interrelationships in the planning hierarchy between mission and objective setting, organizational politics, inputs from stakeholders and corporate culture.

Part 2: External Analysis

4. **Business and Economic analysis**
   Arenas of economic change, classifying organizational environments, the scope of environmental scanning, impact analysis systems and techniques.

5. **Structural (Industry) analysis** *Porters*
   Structural analysis and competitive strategy, changes in domestic and international markets, global hospitality /tourism trends and implications.

6. **Competitor analysis**
   Competitive advantage and generic marketing strategies, retailing concepts, development options and the role of branding and franchising in expansion.

Part 3: Internal Analysis

7. **Portfolio analysis**
   The use of strategic models in portfolio analysis, applying generic models to strategic planning tasks and the role of case analysis in performance reviews.

8. **Operations analysis**
   Systems design and interrelationships between quality, productivity and profitability, performance improvement and assuring operational standards.

9. **Resource analysis**
   Value chain analysis, productivity options, financial performance appraisal, generic productivity strategies and resource management implications.

Part 4: Strategic Choice

10. **Generating and evaluating options**
    Creative thinking and problem solving techniques, generating strategic options and applying risk appraisal techniques to identify optimal strategic fit.

11. **Strategies for change**
    Devising and implementing strategies for specific business needs (turnaround, consolidation, growth), identifying the structural implications of expansion.

12. **Planning for change**
    The characteristics of organizational change, initiating change, appraising the impact of change on the corporate culture and on business performance.

Part 5: Strategic Implementation and Evaluation

13. **Monitoring business strategy**
    Implementing and monitoring business strategy, a process-based model for evaluating business performance, the role of control and regulatory systems.

14. **Achieving structure and strategy co-alignment**
    Managing the interface between external change and the internal structures, processes, procedures and strategies used by the organization.

15. **Sustaining strategic focus**
    The strategic role of total quality management in organizational development and growth and in overall process and performance improvement.

RATIONALE

All organizations, whether large or small must make decisions about the nature of the activity in which they wish to engage, the goals they seek to achieve and the overall direction they want to pursue. After this, they must consider how to plan and co-ordinate their activities and make best use of resources, meet customer needs, compete effectively, monitor performance and review their achievements. In order to do all of this, organizations must devise structures that define task-related boundaries, processes for making decisions and procedures to carry them out. As the decisions are made, implemented, monitored and controlled, the decision-makers need to think strategically so as to assess the wider implications of their actions for the organization as a whole.

Michael D. Olsen, one of America's top academics in the field of strategic management, asserts that the most significant management issue facing hospitality /tourism firms in the 1990s is the need to convert operations-oriented unit-level managers into strategic-thinking managers. This opinion on the challenge facing both industry and education coincides with our view that strategic management is a vitally important perspective for all managers.

RESOURCES

The following publications constitute the resource on which this book is based:

A   R. Teare & A. Boer (eds.) *Strategic Hospitality Management: Theory and Practice for the 1990s.* Cassell, London & New York, 1991. Pb. £14.99 ($24.95) ISBN 0-304-32285-7.

B   N. M. Glass, *Pro-Active Management: How to Improve Your Management Performance.* Cassell, London & Nichols, New Jersey, 1991. Pb £12.99, ISBN 0-304-33006-X.

C   C. Gore, K. Murray, B. Richardson, *Strategic Decision-Making.* Cassell, London & New York, 1992. Pb £15.99 ($24.95) ISBN 0-304-31965-1.

D   R. Teare with D. Adams & S. Messenger (eds.) *Managing Projects in Hospitality Organizations.* Cassell, London & New York, 1992. Pb £15.99 ($24.95) ISBN 0-304-32505-8.

E   R. Teare & M. D. Olsen (eds.) *International Hospitality Management: Corporate Strategy in Practice.* Pitman, London & John Wiley, New York, 1992. Pb £19.99, ISBN 0-471-57099-0.

F   R. Teare with L. Moutinho & N. Morgan (eds.) *Managing and Marketing Services in the 1990s.* Cassell, London & New York, 1993. Pb £12.99 ($24.95) ISBN 0-304-32726-3.

G   R. Teare, C. Atkinson & C. Westwood (eds.) *Achieving Quality Performance: Lessons from British Industry,* Cassell, London & New York, 1993. Pb £13.99 ($24.95) ISBN 0-304-32758-1.

H   M. D. Olsen, E. C. Y. Tse & J. J. West, *Strategic Management in the Hospitality Industry,* ITP, Andover, Hants & VNR, New York, 1992. Hb. £37.00, ISBN 0-442-00246-7.

- *International Journal of Contemporary Hospitality Management* (IJCHM) MCB University Press, Bradford, Yorkshire. ISSN 0959-6119 (published six times a year).

All references to the resource publications are cited in abbreviated form. For example:

- Chapter 2 in *Strategic Hospitality Management* is cited as A: 2 pp 9-30.
- Articles published in the *International Journal of Contemporary Hospitality Management* are cited by author, volume, number, year, and page number(s) e.g. M.D.Olsen, IJCHM, v1n2, 1989 p.6.

To undertake the extension work at the end of each chapter, access to publications: **D** and **G** is essential:

Managing Projects in Hospitality Organizations covers a wide range of hospitality and tourism project settings, including: contract and transport services, employee feeding, fast-food restaurant operations, food production, hospital and local authority services, hotels and tourism development.

Achieving Quality Performance features detailed analysis of six award-winning British companies, namely: Amersham International, Campbell Lee Computer Services, Hydrapower Dynamics, ICL, Land Rover and Prudential Assurance. These case examples illustrate some of the many approaches to continuous improvement and quality management adopted by British Industry in recent years.

We would like to express our thanks to Rachel and Rowena for their love and support.

Richard Teare, Hadyn Ingram
September, 1994

Richard Teare is Professor & Associate Head, Department of Service Industries, Bournemouth University. He is Editor of the *International Journal of Contemporary Hospitality Management*, Associate Editor of *International Marketing Review* and a non-executive director of the National Society for Quality through Teamwork.

Hadyn Ingram is a Senior Lecturer in the Department of Service Industries, Bournemouth University. He holds an MSc from Oxford Brookes University and he has extensive senior management experience in the hotel and public house sectors of the hospitality industry.

1 STRUCTURES

INTRODUCTION

Structure generally refers to the way in which organizations arrange capital and human resources to accomplish their goals. It also defines the authority and communication channels and how resource allocation is to be co-ordinated and controlled. Structures are influenced by internal relationships, managerial styles and strategic decision making, particularly with regard to the degree of formality (rules and regulations), centralization (of power and control) and complexity (extent of specialization) that exists within the organization:

"For an organization to compete in a mature and competitive environment over the long range it must be able to match these structural variables with activities and trends occurring in the environment."
(M.D.Olsen, IJCHM, v1n2, 1989, p.3.)

In this chapter:
- Characteristics of organizational structures (B: 11 pp 44-47; C: 4 pp 67-72)
- Centralization or decentralization? (A: 2 pp 21-25; C: 4 pp 71-72)
- Models of structure (C: 4 pp 72-78)
- M-form organizational structure (C: 4 pp 79-85)
- Forte PLC: The impact of growth on an M-form structure (A: 1 pp 3-6)
- Organizational design in the global environment (E: 11 pp 181-194)

REVIEW

Characteristics of organizational structures
(B: 11 pp 44-47; C: 4 pp 67-72)
An organization's structure should assist employees to achieve pre-determined objectives. This means that the structure should provide a mechanism for organizing resources, clarifying roles and responsibilities, shaping an effective decision-making process and facilitating two-way communication between managers and their staff. All structures represent a compromise between two opposing pressures; centralized control of authority and decision-making and a more open, trusting approach to the decentralization of authority. In practice, the political dimension of organizational life means that people generally construct elaborate informal systems to circumnavigate official channels if they are perceived to be unworkable or too bureaucratic (see chapter 3).

Organizational structures can be classified according to a number of characteristic features. These emanate from three different types of structure:
- *Classical* - a military style 'command and control' structure, characterized by a strict hierarchy, clearly defined roles and responsibilities for each level, formal procedures and relationships and unity of command (meaning that each person has only one direct superior). This type of structure effectively limits the freedom and discretion of the individual and in this way, creativity, innovation and individualism are discouraged.
- *Behavioural* - places greater emphasis upon personal responsibility and participation in decision making and this tends to stimulate creativity and greater commitment to organizational goals. A common way of achieving wider involvement is by adopting a policy of decentralization and creating semi-autonomous strategic business units (SBU's) and profit centres.
- *Contingency* - a theoretical argument in support of the view that there is no single correct structure and that an organization should adapt its structure according to the prevailing conditions and circumstances. Key determinants are the nature of the work or task, the people who will perform it and the environment in which they operate (B: 11 p.46). Contingency theory highlights the need for co-existing structures within one organization so as to embrace different functions, each with different goals, time horizons, types of people and working practices. Organizations should seek to differentiate activities according to style and structure characteristics and, at the same time, promote integration so that differentiated functions can work co-operatively.

Classical (or formal) organizational structures can also be described as 'mechanistic' because they operate like a machine with fully elaborated operating procedures for every task and job role. Burns and Stalker (1) argue that this type of structure is insufficiently flexible to cope with anything other than stable market conditions. A more informal and adaptive structure is needed to compete in continually changing market conditions. Burns and Stalker refer to this as an 'organic' structure, characterized by a high level of interaction between employees, effective group and team-working and emphasis on the importance of the individual.

Centralization or decentralization?
(A: 2 pp 21-25; C: 4 pp 71-72)
It is generally assumed that formal organizations are characterized by centralized decision-making, informal by a decentralized structure. However, the strategic behaviour of an organization is frequently influenced by the dynamic combination of product-market changes (strategy) evolving structures and processes and an array of other factors. It is possible to map some of the key combinations affecting structural change using typologies of strategic behaviour:
- *Miles and Snow* identify three key market positions - (a) protect current market share, (b) protect current market share and locate new opportunities, (c) locate new product and market opportunities, each with different implications for strategy, structure and minimizing risk. (see Table 2.1; A: 2 p. 22.)
- *Campbell and Gould* identify three senior management styles - (a) financial control, (b) strategic control, (c) strategic planning, each with implications for the preferred type of organizational structure and the extent to which decision making is likely to be centralized (Figure 2.3; A: 2 p. 24).
- *Hassard* developed a two dimensional matrix to examine styles of strategic behaviour. The matrix plots development strategy (the extent to which policy-making is centralized or decentralized) against control strategies to identify four generic styles - (a) navigator, (b) banker, (c) gambler, (d) strategist (Figure 2.4; A: 2 p. 25).

Models of structure (C: 4 pp 72-78)
The way in which an organization is structured can normally be determined from the hierarchy and interrelationships depicted on an organizational chart. By comparing the common features of charts, it is possible to identify the basis for modelling different types of structure. The main types of structures are as follows:
- *Simple* - typically small businesses with a high degree of informal networking and personal interaction between the owner(s) and employees.
- *Functional* - describes a company organization based on the areas of specialization and expertise such as accounting, marketing, operations and personnel. This provides a number of efficiency advantages linked to gains from economies of specialization.
- *Holding company* - meaning an investment company holding a portfolio of shares (see Figure 4.2; p. 74) or a parent company with independent businesses, often with independent names. The primary role of a holding company is buying (acquiring) and selling (divesting) businesses that collectively represent a portfolio of related or unrelated business interests, independently assessed according to their performance (see chapter 7).
- *Multidivisional structure* - is used to organize business activities in accordance with defined markets, services/products and related factors (see Figure 4.3). This provides a specialized business focus and facilitates unit performance measurement so that profit differentials for different markets and products can be monitored more easily.

M-form organizational structure (C: 4 pp 79-85)
Empirical evidence shows that large firms in particular, have tended to implement change by developing a structure based on divisions. This is now the dominant organizational form. A key issue in setting up and developing such a structure is the extent to which a division should be autonomous. An M-form firm is multidivisional, characterized by decentralized decision-making closely linked to financial accountability. Each division acts as a profit centre which can be monitored and assessed by head office according to its performance. In turn, this facilitates more objective resource allocation so that the profitable divisions can expand and further improve their contribution to the organization as a whole. In this way, the firm is operating as an internal capital market whereby the allocation of resources is determined on the basis of an objective analysis of performance.

Forte: The impact of growth on an M-form structure (A: 1 pp 3-6)
Strategic planning in large organizations is not a static process, it evolves as the size and structure of the company changes:

"Fifteen years ago the process was different, and strategy was formulated almost exclusively at the centre. The chief executive made investment decisions and then delegated responsibility for integrating new acquisitions into the company. A different approach is needed today because the company is much larger and operates in a number of sectors. Consequently, it is no longer possible for one individual at the centre to focus in sufficient detail on every aspect of the business. The strategic thrust of the company therefore comes from a dialogue between the centre and the operating divisions, which prepare their own strategic plans. The plans then form the basis of a discussion from which a corporate plan is constructed." (p. 3.)

A policy of decentralizing authority and responsibility for decision-making has helped to create strong divisional teams and to balance the move towards greater divisional autonomy:

"When the company was smaller, the issue of financing new development was less contentious, but as strategic planning is now a divisional responsibility, more ambitious development plans are emerging...As a direct consequence of this, corporate aims and objectives are continually monitored to determine where the company should be heading and what the emphasis for the future should be. These considerations determine when and how changes to the product portfolio are made. All of these issues will influence the direction and structure of the company during the 1990s because it cannot sustain growth in every division at the same time and at the same pace." (p. 5.)

Accordingly, key questions used by Forte for determining levels of support for divisional expansion include: (a) What is the maximum potential of each operation? (b) How do we reach the point where we are realizing this potential if we decide to support development? (c) How much will the development cost? (d) How quickly can we penetrate the market to achieve market leadership?

Organizational design in the global environment
(E: 11 pp 181-194)
There are many complex considerations arising from expanding across national boundaries (see also chapter 11) but perhaps the most critical in so far as establishing an appropriate structure, are the design considerations. Farber and Probasco identify six key design criteria for hospitality/tourism organizations:

Alignment with foreign environments.
Prior to expanding internationally, the organization must identify benefits that add value to the firm. Central to this is the need for a careful evaluation of the degree of difficulty associated with aligning with a foreign environment. Key considerations are securing the requisite resource inputs, work process efficiencies and sources of consumption for the output of products and services.

Ownership patterns and contractual arrangements.
A key issue to resolve prior to overseas expansion is the appropriate mode of entry and level of ownership. These vary from high ownership/risk to low ownership risk: (a) full ownership, (b) holding company with subsidiaries owning/part-owning assets, (c) joint ventures where the division of ownership is agreed upon by the two or more parties involved, (d) a management company to operate but not wholly own property real estate, (e) franchise systems providing methods, technical assistance and marketing to investors.

There are other factors to take into consideration such as political stability and the attitude of host country governments to foreign investment. It may be advantageous to enter contractual relationships with overseas investors - EuroDisney is a case in point (see p. 184).

Societal authority systems.
Market entry in a host country may require a careful study of the way in which systems of authority and power operate, so that cross-cultural differences can be reconciled with organizational design. In general, American firms regard organizations as sociocultural systems that need to be flexible in structure. This helps to explain why multinational corporations like McDonald's permit decentralized decision-making throughout their worldwide network. However, firms originating elsewhere in the world often exhibit a different style of management, and attempts to impose structures and decision-making processes modelled on home markets may impede success.

Resource availability.
To sustain organizations in host markets, appropriate host country resource infrastructures are needed. To secure sources of supply at the requisite quality level, linkages with local agencies and supply lines may be needed, ranging from the creation or acquisition of local firms to the establishment of joint ventures with local suppliers.

Comparative modes of compartmentalization.
As hospitality/tourism organizations grow and expand overseas, the issue of how they compartmentalize their activities affects subsequent development. There are principally eight design considerations which should be reviewed in order to create an appropriate structure for each host country. These are: complexity, specialization, hierarchy of authority, standardization, formalization, professionalization, centralization and personnel ratios. It is the host country that most markedly affects levels of professionalization, centralization of decision making and personnel ratios for hotel and restaurant operations.

Critical internal and external interdependencies.
As noted above, multinational hospitality/tourism organizations are likely to adopt different structures according to host country trading, economic, social and political conditions. This gives rise to a vast network of interdependencies or linkages between the firm, its divisions (home and host countries) and the external environment. Arising from this is the prospect of achieving beneficial forms of integration within the organization as a whole.

CONCLUSION

The variety of possible configurations would suggest that organizations should seek to design structures which satisfy internal priorities and/or prevailing market conditions. It is unlikely however, that any one type of structure is sufficiently adaptable to cope with changing internal and external circumstances.

Daft (2) outlines a number of steps for creating or reviewing and adapting organizational design (E: 11 p. 177):
- Develop organization charts that describe task responsibilities, reporting relationships and work groups;
- Provide vertical and horizontal information linkages so as to integrate diverse departments within a coherent whole;
- Choose between functional or product-related structures when designing the overall organizational structure;
- Implement hybrid structures, when needed, in large firms by dividing the organization into self-contained product groups and assigning each function needed for the product line to the product division;
- Consider a matrix structure in certain organization settings if neither the product nor the functional structure works effectively;
- Consider a structural reorganization whenever the symptoms of structural deficiency are observed.

References:

1. T.Burns and G.M.Stalker. *The Management of Innovation.* Tavistock, London, 1961.
2. R.L.Daft. *Organization Theory and Design.* West Publishing, St. Paul, MN, 1989.

Review questions:

1. Review the organizational structure of your placement firm or a firm with which you are familiar and determine its characteristic features.

2. With reference to the typologies of strategic behaviour, explain the factors influencing the adoption of centralized and decentralized structures.

3. Identify the differences between 'U-form' and 'M-form' firms using industry examples to explain the respective merits of each.

EXTENSION

Read: Chapter 5 of *Managing Projects in Hospitality Organizations* (D: 5 pp 129-145).

The chapter provides an overview of the development and introduction of an new catering, planning, accounting and control (CATPAC) system in the Army Catering Service. The cultural and organizational characteristics typify a classical structure and the implementation of the CATPAC project acted as a catalyst for organizational change, particularly in relation to power and authority relationships within work groups.

Extension questions:

1. Hierarchical organizations are often considered to be rigid, inflexible and resistant to change. Why did the catering organization respond to the changes imposed by the CATPAC system?

2. Information often equates with power in organizational terms. Evaluate the strategic impact of CATPAC as an information system for senior management.

3. Identify the changes to the organizational culture of the catering work group following the introduction of the CATPAC system. Why did these changes occur? Were they beneficial?

Practical exercises:

1. Select a large hospitality/tourism firm and using published information sources, study the changes that have been made to its organizational structure over a period of at least five years. Identify the reasons for changes and comment on the implications.

2. Compare and contrast large and small hospitality/tourism firms with which you are familiar commenting on the relative strengths and weaknesses of their organizational structures.

3. Design a structure to improve the organization of a college/university and its portfolio of courses. Comment on the criteria you have used and explain how they have influenced your design. Review the expected benefits and drawbacks in the context of current educational opportunities and constraints.

2
PROCESSES

INTRODUCTION

"Good managers are aware of the process of strategic decision-making, and they consciously intervene in it. They use it to improve the information available for decisions and to build the psychological identification essential to successful strategies...properly managed, it is a conscious, purposeful, pro-active executive practice."
J.B.Quinn, *Strategies for Change.* Irwin. New York. 1980.

Strategic management embodies the work of many authors who have attempted to explain the plans and actions which contribute to corporate success. Strategic processes are the mechanisms by which effective strategic management comes about. They are often supported by frameworks which assist in the difficult practice of decision-making. It is the task of the manager to make decisions, which are affected by both management style and the culture of the business organization.

In this chapter:
- The role of the manager (B: 2 pp 6-9)
- Management style (B: 3 pp 10-14)
- Decision-making defined (C: 1 pp 1-2)
- Levels of decision-making (C: 1 pp 2-4)
- Rational decision-making (C: 1 pp 4-8)
- Strategic decision model processes (C: 1 pp 8-11)
- Criticism of the models (C: 1 pp 12-13)
- Practical considerations (C: 1 pp 18-19)
- What is strategy? (C: 7 pp 138-145 & H: 2 pp 16-40)
- Generic strategies (C: 7 pp 141-145)
- Formulating strategy (C: 7 pp 146-147)
- Corporate fit (A: 2 pp 19- 21)

REVIEW

The role of the manager (B: 2 pp 6-9)
Managers have traditionally adopted the autocratic role of planning, organizing and controlling the work and the workforce. Social and technological changes have influenced the function of management, especially where the pace of business life has increased from a stable to a more dynamic environment. The effective managers of the future will need to be:

- facilitators
- conflict resolvers
- coordinators

Management style (B: 3 pp 10-14)
Much research has been undertaken in the search for the ultimate management style. The behavioural approach concentrates on the manager's interaction with subordinates while contingency models favour a style which is appropriate to the needs of the organization. Clearly, a manager's style is shaped by his own personality, the organization (and its workforce) and the environment in which it operates.

Decision-making defined (C: 1 pp 1-2)
Whichever style is adopted, one of the prime responsibilities of management is to make decisions. For the modern business organization ensuring that decision-making is effective is extremely important. Effective decision-making enables companies to achieve their objectives in an efficient manner and provides a means of establishing operating and control systems.

But what is a decision?
It could be said that a decision is a rational process composed of a number of distinctive stages. It is preceded by a conscious evaluation and choice between alternatives for meeting an objective, even if the alternative chosen is to do nothing. A non-choice option is frequently selected to avoid conflict and to maintain the status quo.

Levels of decision-making (C: 1 pp 2-4)
The activity of decision-making can be divided into classes of decisions. One such taxonomy is provided by Simon (1):
- *Programmed decisions* are repetitive and routine, utilizing decision criteria derived from past performance and experience.
- *Non-programmed decisions* are unique and complex; they require judgement and creativity, since they are characterized by incomplete information and uncertainty.

Another classification is offered by Ansoff (2):
- *Strategic decisions* are concerned with objectives and long range plans, which are usually the province of top management.
- *Administrative decisions* are usually taken by middle management and are concerned with aspects of organizational control, systems and motivation.
- *Operating decisions* are normally adopted by lower management, these are routine decisions which are constrained by rules, methods and procedures.

Although different levels of decision-making are identified by various writers, in practice it is often difficult to distinguish between the levels.

Rational decision-making (C: 1 pp 4-8)
A decision could be described as rational if it is based upon a logical process, using the best available information to achieve a particular end or objective.

The search for rationality in economic theory demands:
- An economic objective which can be quantified and that reflects the objectives of the decision-maker.
- Consistent preferences of decision-makers for their objectives.
- Unlimited information-processing capabilities by those involved and an ability to maximize their own self-interest and act accordingly.
- Well defined, mutually exclusive alternatives.
- Accurate and quantified estimates of the expected value of each alternative.
- Selection of the alternative that maximizes 'expected utility'.
- Unlimited information and no time or cost constraints.

In the real world, such perfect rationality cannot be achieved because objectives are not always simple - preferences change and cognitive ability is circumscribed by the limits of human brain power. As a complete evaluation of all possibilities can never be carried out, optimal solutions to complex problems cannot always be found and rationality is limited or 'bounded' by circumstances (1).

Strategic decision-model processes (C: 1 pp 11)
The stages involved in decision-making processes mentioned by writers are: set objectives; problem recognition; problem definition; information gathering (search); develop alternatives (diagnosis); evaluate alternatives; choice; implementation; monitor (follow up).

Criticism of the models (C: 1 pp 12-13)
- A model provides a construction of reality influenced by the intentions and preferences of its builder.
- Models should embody theories which explain practices, thus neither theory nor practice should be viewed without recourse to the other.

Hofer and Schendel (3) suggest a process for formulating strategy based upon the notion of bounded rationality. The stages are:

- Goal formulation;
- Strategy formulation - (a) issue identification; (b) formulate alternatives; (c) evaluate alternatives; (d) choice;
- Implementation.

According to Higgins (4) the main issue is the identification of information needs. Accordingly, strategic objectives should be compared with required performance and the corporate plan, individual business plans and operational budgets.

Mintzberg (5) on the other hand, suggests that because of bounded rationality the process is not sequential, but involves considerable back-tracking or repetition of stages. Consequently, there is no firm distinction between the levels of decision-making. He claims that actual decision processes fall into three stages:
- Identification - recognition and diagnosis of the existing problem and causal factors.
- Development - search for solutions drawing upon the organization's experience and knowledge and dividing the problem into smaller parts.
- Selection - screening to eliminate unfeasible solutions, followed by evaluation and choice.

Practical considerations (C: 1 pp 18-19)
What practical reasons are there for studying strategic decision processes? An analysis of the way decisions are taken within an organization (breaking the process into stages) makes it possible to compare the model produced with an idealized model. In this way, is easier to suggest specific improvements at particular points or stages. The interrelationships between the stages can be considered, so that management can review the functioning of the decision-making process as a whole.

Models of management strategy aid the process of strategic decision-making and act as sensitizing concepts. They indicate areas for thought and investigation so as to facilitate the making of better decisions. Rather than providing prescriptions of what to do or what to see, many of the models of management strategy merely suggest directions in which to look.

What is strategy? (C: 7 pp138-145 & H: 2 pp16-40)
There is a lack of consensus on the precise meaning and role of strategy but it is generally agreed that:
- *Strategy personifies the organization.* Strategy is fundamentally concerned with the mechanisms for creating wealth and for achieving profit generating objectives, distributing wealth and providing satisfaction to stakeholders.

- *Strategy is the means by which the organization adapts to the environment in which it operates.* The fundamental task of strategic management is to enable the organization to adapt in the face of changing opportunities and threats.
- *Strategy is an integral part of the organization's planning system.* Strategy represents a systemized pattern of decisions relating to objectives or goals, and the ways of achieving those goals. Improvements in information technology are enabling operational management information systems to be replaced by strategic decision support systems. Systems such as yield management assist hospitality managers to make optimal capacity and price decisions. (P.R.Gamble, IJCHM, v2 n1, 1990, pp 4-9.)

Generic strategies (C: 7 pp 141-145)
Generic strategies are particular sets of plans for particular types of problems, nine of which follow:
- *Political strategies.* General strategies focusing on people (groups) as a means of achieving action.
- *Corporate planning strategies.* Those plans and decisions relating to major long term organizational developments which seek to establish the position of the firm in the marketplace.
- *Competitive strategies.* The making of plans and decisions to enhance organizational competitiveness.
- *Contingency strategies.* Strategies which take account of risk and uncertainty in changing environmental situations.
- *Administrative strategies.* The making of effective administrative plans and decisions.
- *Team contribution strategies.* Those concerned with the creation of organization-wide team effort, involving all personnel at all levels, in all functions and in virtually everything.
- *Productivity strategies.* The conception of plans designed to improve significantly the wealth-producing productivity and performance of the organization.
- *Innovation strategies.* Those tactics which may enhance organizational creativity (thinking up new product and process ideas) and innovation (putting new ideas, successfully into practice).
- *Shock event strategies.* The anticipation of what might otherwise have been major shocks (crisis management) or unforeseen opportunities and the effective response to them when they happen. In a word, planning the unplannable.

All these plans revolve around the management strategists, who work at the centre of the organization and control the strategic planning system.

Formulating strategy (C: 7 pp 146-147)
Strategy-making is concerned with the resolution of problems related to the achievement of objectives, and uses knowledge from a range of disciplines. Strategy cannot be based upon 'recipes' as it is continuously evolving and management strategy remains a user-specific, situation-specific concept.

Linear sequential decision-making represents traditional 'top-down' strategy formulation, but Minzberg (5) notes that an increasing number of organizations seek consultation and participation from different levels, thereby generating what he terms *emergent* strategy. Strategic management is a complex phenomena which changes over time, often in an *incremental* way. The rational, systematic models of decision-making are sometimes criticized for failing to take account of enterpreneurial or intuitive skills, but they can be used to provide structure to managerial checklists, often devised in the quest for effective strategy:

"...in general the (strategic) models are too simplistic...(but) it is their very simplicity that makes the models so useful. Dangers can arise when one follows the models too closely, not making allowance for the dynamics of one's industry or by expecting the models to provide the answers to questions; a good model will only lead you to seek the right information and ask the right question."
(D.J.W.Fender, IJCHM, v2 n3, 1990, p vi.)

Corporate fit (A: 2 pp 19-21)
This logical process of decision-making must be in keeping with the organization's corporate culture, that is the shared beliefs, assumptions and values of all members of the organization. Corporate culture is constantly changing and may be influenced and manipulated by power groups, affecting attitudes towards risk, centralized control and acceptable performance levels in the organization.

CONCLUSION

All managers have an important part to play in the conception and implementation of coherent strategies for their companies. Models of decision-making in the strategic planning process are valuable tools in maximizing the effects of the decision, despite the constraints on perfect rationality.

Generic strategies are available to cope with particular types of problems, but the decisions taken and the process by which they are decided must be in keeping with the culture of the organization. In reality, strategic management may well be a logical and sequential process, but the effective strategist will be aware that it incorporates social, political and cultural perspectives.

Review questions:

1. What are the requirements for rational decision-making to take place? Can those requirements ever be achieved in practice?

2. Write notes on each stage in the strategic decision-making process and identify from your own observations, experience and further reading, which stages are the most important and why.

3. Which (if any) generic strategies should hospitality organizations have in place, and in what circumstances could they play a part?

References:

1. H.A.Simon, *The New Science of Management Decision.* Harper & Row, New York, 1987, pp 25.
2. H.I.Ansoff, *Business Strategy.* Penguin, Harmondsworth, 1969.
3. C.W.Hofer and D. Schendel, *Strategy Formulation: Analytical Concepts.* West Publishing, St. Paul, MN. 1978.
4. J.C.Higgins, 'Management information systems for corporate planning.' in *Corporate Strategy and Planning,* B.Taylor and J.R.Sparkes (eds), Heinemann, London, 1982; pp 299-310.
5. H.Minzberg, 'Crafting Strategy', *Harvard Business Review,* July/August 1987; pp 66-75.

EXTENSION

Read: Chapter 3 of *Managing Projects in Hospitality Organizations* (D: 3 pp 77-100).

The chapter follows the process of compulsory competitive tendering for domestic services in the National Health Service from inception through to full contract implementation. It reviews the role of government, trade unions, competition and employment issues, explains the mechanics and practical implications of undertaking such an exercise and considers the impact of organizational change on hospital staff and patients.

Extension questions:

1. Identify the stages in the strategic decision-making process for competitive tendering in the National Health Service. Prepare a conceptual model of the process and identify the critical stages. What are the constraints to producing an effective outcome?

2. Suggest who the major stakeholders are in the competitive tendering procedure and plot their areas of influence diagrammatically. Suggest ways in which stakeholder disruption might be minimized.

3. Draw up a competitive tendering document defining costs, implementation methods and control/monitoring procedures for a specific service requirement (e.g. based on service specifications for a college reception/foyer). The tender should be accurately costed in terms of manpower and materials prior to presentation to group members who will critically evaluate both the process and the probable outcome of the proposal.

Practical exercises:

1. Review a major business decision you have had to take, in an objective and analytical way. Using a sequential model, comment critically upon each stage of the process and suggest ways in which improvements may have been made in order to produce a better outcome.

2. Debate the advantages and disadvantages of the 'scientific' approaches to strategic management. Is this approach appropriate to all types of organization and management styles?

3. With reference to an organization with which you are familiar, write notes on the decision processes within that organization. Identify the decision-makers and those stakeholders who could influence the decisions. Comment upon the style of management and its effect upon the quality of the decision and those who were required to implement it.

4. 'The incremental approach to decision-making is the only one to adopt in the current business climate.' Debate this statement citing examples of strategies adopted by hospitality organizations in support of your arguments.

3
PROCEDURES

INTRODUCTION

Strategic planning, whether formalized as in large organizations or more informally addressed in small firms, requires a sense of strategic purpose, direction and vision so that business activity can be properly focused and optimized. This implies the existence of goals or objectives to guide the formulation and implementation of strategy and provide measures against which performance can be assessed. Accordingly, effective strategic planning requires an understanding of the procedures which can be used to put ideas into practice and an appreciation of the planning influences and interrelationships as represented by the differing interpretations of stakeholders - the many groups of people with a vested interest in the success of the organization.

In this chapter:
- The strategic planning hierarchy of organizational objectives (C: 2 pp 25-32; 37-48)
- Power in organizations (B: 15 pp 59-62; C: 2 pp 36-37)
- Organizations as political systems (B: 14 pp 56-58)
- Organizational stakeholders (C: 4 pp 33-37)
- Corporate culture (B: 13 pp 52-55; C: 3 pp 49-64)
- Integrating organizational structures, processes and procedures (E: 14 pp 228-254)

REVIEW

The strategic planning hierarchy of organizational objectives (C: 2 pp 25-32; 37-48)
The many theories about organizational or corporate objectives tend to assume that the owners or managers of the firm are in control, seek profit maximization and/or the success of other objectives on behalf of stakeholders (see Table 2.1 p. 28). The ability to act is influenced by the corporate culture, organizational and power structures and by the management styles of decision-makers.

Argenti (1) defines the mission statement as a declaration of purpose, a *raison d'etre* with explicit reference to its long term survival and promotion of stakeholder interests. Three example extracts from mission statements help to illustrate this (p. 31):

(a) *Constantly seeking ways of improving the total service to customers.*
(b) *To grow profitably on a worldwide scale through aggressive marketing of high quality branded foods.*
(c) *Profits, growth in a free market economy, quality of products and service to customers, respect for the dignity and worth of individuals, provision of equal opportunities and the desire to be good world citizens.*

To translate mission into measurable objectives, a cascading mechanism is needed so that an interdependent hierarchy of objectives can be constructed, appropriate to every level of business activity. This form of business procedure is commonly referred to as *management by objectives* (MBO), starting with the organization's mission which is translated into corporate level strategic objectives and then to business or operational level objectives. MBO attempts to align operational objectives set for the component parts of a firm with the strategic objectives. To work, it requires clear, firm but sensitive leadership, effective two-way communication channels and personnel policy that ensures the harmonious operation of selection, training and reward systems.

Power in organizations
(B: 15 pp 59-62; C: 2 pp 36-37)
Power is a relational concept which is used to achieve certain outcomes, based on an individual's perception of serving their own and/or the organization's best interests. The negative connotations of power emanate from its misuse, and from the manipulation of people's perceptions via persuasion or coercion. There are many sources of power in organizations and the way in which it is used depends upon the individual's awareness of its existence, possession, skill at control, tactical abilities and personality (traits such as courage, ambition, willingness to use power, ethics). Power is most constructive when it is applied openly and legitimately and when it is carefully targeted to promote the company's interests rather than to further personal ambition.

Organizations as political systems
(B: 14 pp 56-58)
As noted in chapter 1, organizations tend to develop unique and distinctive political systems within which different factions engage in a struggle for power and influence. Political behaviour is also motivated by competition for scarce resources such as budgets, people, tasks, territory, status, power and technology. Factions form around a number of axes or key interests such as issues (e.g. should the organization grow?) functions (e.g. sales vs. production)

hierarchy, tradition and size (e.g. small vs. large departments). Interest groups possess different goals, time-orientations and values and exhibit different behavioural styles and language use.

Organizational change is one of the main catalysts of organizational activity and four main factions may emerge; (a) those who previously held power, may feel threatened and are inclined to resist change, (b) those who believe in the need for change, (c) those who don't care either way, (d) those who felt unhappy before and support change in the hope of gaining advantages from it. Additionally, factions may combine their efforts in an effort to maintain the status quo. If they succeed, the organization's ability to adapt will be weakened. This type of political activity is sometimes referred to as 'dynamic conservatism' as it describes a desire to adapt which is impeded by resistance to change.

Although politics cannot be separated from organizational life, there are ways in which the energy it generates can be harnessed. First, it is essential to develop an overall organizational strategy that is realistic, yet challenging, straightforward and comprehensible. Each department should then develop its own strategy for contributing to and helping to achieve the overall organizational strategy. In this way, energy is focused upon achieving common goals with individual outcomes that can be measured, recognized and rewarded in an appropriate way.

Organizational stakeholders (C: 4 pp 33-37)
A stakeholder is an individual who belongs to a group of people or institutions with a common interest in a particular organization. Stakeholder groups and respective principal interests are typically: *shareholders* (dividends, capital gains); *managers* (salaries, job satisfaction, promotion); *employees* (wages, security, conditions); *customers* (good products and service); *suppliers* (orders and steady demand); *lenders* (interest payable at low risk); *society* (taxes and corporate responsibility).

A key responsibility of management is to reconcile the conflicting claims and interests of stakeholders. Further, with reference to the various needs and expectations of stakeholder groups, a periodic review of each group's ability to exert power and influence on objective setting and decision-making may help to anticipate the likelihood of power struggles occurring between two or more groups.

Summarizing, the relationships between corporate mission, objectives and stakeholders can be expressed as follows:

"Strategic vision represents the organization's long-term aspiration of what it can become and do and what it will not attempt. Beliefs about capital-market expectations are concerned with what it will take to keep investors and other stakeholders satisfied. Beliefs about product-market expectations are concerned with how and why the organization can succeed in its industry...Together these beliefs cover a range of topics: from what financial goals should be, how marketing is done, what are acceptable risks, what planning, control, and co-ordination devices will work best for an organization, what managing really encompasses, ideal internal structures, preferred technologies, the best set of employee inducements, acceptable competitor and union-management relationships, appropriate public service and community support, and so on."
(C.Lundberg & R.Woods, IJCHM, v2n4, 1990, p.6.)

A diagrammatic representation of how one company sought to reconcile conflicting stakeholder interests is shown in Figure 2. 5 (p.36). The overall mission emphasises the creation of wealth and illustrates the benefits that accrue for each of the key stakeholder groups.

Corporate culture (B: 13 pp 52-55; C: 3 pp 49-64)
An organization's culture is closely linked its ethos, mission and type of structure and because of this, it permeates every aspect of organization life:

"At the core of any organizational culture are the organization-specific values, assumptions and associated ideologies which constitute its essential character. These typically unconscious and invisible taken-for-granted premises and precepts generally determine how members perceive, think and learn."
(C.Lundberg & R.Woods, IJCHM, v2n4, 1990, p.6.)

Culture also encompasses the set of attitudes, styles and behaviours of the organization as personified by the freedom given to individuals, the way people communicate and work, the surroundings they work in and the kinds of people who are successful. The following mission statement extract illustrates a desire to shape these variables in a positive and productive way, by seeking to build and sustain an organizational culture which encourages and rewards employees for their individual and collective efforts:

"Our aim is always to help and encourage individuals to develop their skills and responsibilities, enabling them to build rewarding careers within our environment where quality and teamwork go hand in hand." Scott's Hotels Limited.

As noted above, stakeholder groups generally have different perspectives on corporate objectives and priorities and these may be reflected in different norms of behaviour, value systems and beliefs. Interaction between stakeholder groups may lead to the formation of rules of conduct defining acceptable behaviour, sometimes referred to as 'the way we get things done around here'.

Peters and Waterman (2) set out to discover the characteristics or culture of successful companies. They began by using McKinsey's 7-S framework (see Figure 3.3, C: 3 p.56) and advocating emphasis on the so called 'soft S's' (style, skills, staff and shared values) rather than the 'hard S's' (strategy, structure, systems). Their sample of companies, drawn from a wide range of industries, revealed a number of commonly occurring features:

- *Bias for action* - successful firms manage to counter the tendency to conformity and inertia by fostering organizational flexibility, ensuring that managers are highly visible and accessible, solving problems step by step, being willing to experiment, setting tight deadlines and simplifying systems.

- *Close relationships with customers* - successful firms tend to be customer-orientated, focusing on revenue generation (rather than over-emphasizing cost control).

- *Autonomy and entrepreneurship* - successful firms encourage innovation and support new ideas and products by adopting organic, decentralized structures.

- *Productivity through people* - successful firms empower their employees (trust, participation in decision-making) and typically, a senior level commitment to employee development is mirrored throughout the organization. It requires a careful selection procedure for new managers so as to ensure optimum fit with this philosophy, management style and culture.

- *Hands-on, value-led management* - equates with the concept of 'servant leadership' whereby senior management strive to create a stimulating, caring environment through personal attention, persistence and direct intervention. This ensures that 'things happen' is accordance with the beliefs, values and goals of the organization.

- *Sticking to the knitting* - organizations are generally more successful if they stick to the things they do best.

- *Simple form, lean structure* - in essence, complex organizational structures should be avoided.

- *Simultaneous loose-tight properties*. Peters and Waterman found that successful firms were generally tightly controlled but at the same time, autonomy, entrepreneurship and innovation from the 'bottom up' were encouraged.

Integrating organizational structures, processes and procedures (E: 14 pp 228-254)

The day-to-day realities of managing organizations tend to promote a rather myopic view of current priorities and business pressures. Managers have limited time to evaluate the extent to which the processes and procedures they are using work effectively, but as noted in chapter 1, there are many design factors which, in the right combination, create synergistic benefits. This analogy is more commonly used to describe the benefits of business alliances (where combined values are greater than individual worth), but well-integrated planning saves time, facilitates greater clarity of thinking, communicating and action planning.

Nebel and Schaffer set out an example of how to build effective interrelationships between corporate (or business) functional (specialist support) and operational (or strategic business unit) levels for a multidivisional hotel firm (pp 229-231).

Strategic planning involves: (a) assessing the current strategic position of the business; (b) identifying the major strategic opportunities, threats and environmental constraints that the business is likely to face; (c) identifying the principal skills and resources available to build a competitive strategy; (d) identifying the major gaps between the business's current strategic position and the likely opportunities, threats and constraints (pp 231-234). Arising from this, organizational objectives can be set or refined and an overall plan addressing the interface between operations and markets, formulated and implemented in consultation with functional specialists and hotel management teams.

CONCLUSION

The complexity of internal relationships and the need to respond to changes taking place in the external environment means that organizational procedures must be sufficiently robust yet adaptable to sustain many different kinds of business activity:

"Generally, the particular problems which the strategist is faced with in designing any set of planning procedures revolve around: (a) the group who are involved in the process, together with the actual mechanics of the process; (b) the frequency of reviews and consequential formalized change; (c) the

actual nature of change within the organization; (d) the extent to which it should be incremental or global in nature. In plain words, these factors address the who, when and how questions in strategy. It is of the utmost importance to take into account the characteristics of the industry and organization in designing systems. If not, systems run the risk of becoming cumbersome and remote and difficulties may arise when change is required." (D.J.W.Fender & D.Litteljohn, IJCHM, v4n3, 1992 p. i.)

References:

1. J.Argenti. *Corporate Planning.* Allan & Unwin, London, 1968.
2. T.J.Peters and R.H.Waterman. *In Search of Excellence.* Harper & Row, New York, 1982.

Review questions:

1. Analyze a hospitality/tourism organization with which you are familiar with reference to the characteristics of its political and corporate culture and power and authority relationships. What improvements would you recommend to senior management?

2. Using the findings of the Peters and Waterman study on 'excellence' comment on the implications for improving the structures, processes and procedures of your placement organization or an organization with which you are familiar.

3. Devise a series of flow diagrams depicting procedures for planning, monitoring and controlling operations in an organization with which you are familiar. Identify the 'fail points' or blockages and explain how they might be resolved.

EXTENSION

Read: Chapter 1 of *Managing Projects in Hospitality Organizations* (D: 5 pp 5-32).

The chapter focuses upon a client-contractor relationship between Sutcliffe Catering Southern Ltd. and P & O European Ferries. The former company specializes in the provision of contract catering and provides both catering and retail services for the latter, a leading operator in the cross channel ferry business. The service contract relationship between these two companies is made all the more interesting by the fact that they were both divisions of the large and diverse P & O Group at the time.

The first part of the chapter addresses the structure and activities of the P & O Group, the second concentrates on the interrelationships between the two divisions and the third part reviews the plans implemented and benefits derived from the service contract.

Extension questions:

1. Undertake a review of the strengths and weaknesses of the cross channel ferry operations described in the chapter, including the potential opportunities on the existing Portsmouth routes. Prepare an integrated plan to include: production; transportation; preparation and service.

2. Outline the control procedures appropriate to a marine contract services division and explain what, if any, improvements you would recommend in the context of the operations review and management accounting systems as described in the chapter.

3. Compare and contrast the infrastructure on board a passenger ferry with that required to operate a commercial in-flight catering unit.

Practical exercises:

1. Prepare a strategic plan detailing how Sutcliffe might develop the P&OEF contract over the next five years. Include an ordered set of priorities for growth and consider the resource implications. Highlight the financial and organizational implications arising from your proposals and explain how foreseeable problems and opportunities might be addressed.

2. Using the operational and financial data available for the P&OEF/Sutcliffe contract, identify how Sutcliffe might use their ferry catering expertise to obtain new on-shore business. Consider the skills, systems and expertise associated with the current activities and how spare capacity might be fully utilized.

3. A competitor to Sutcliffe Catering is about to form a marine contract services division. You have been asked to formulate an appropriate blueprint for the division, to include a proposed structure and details of operating processes and procedures appropriate to entering a new market area.

4
BUSINESS AND ECONOMIC ANALYSIS

INTRODUCTION

"Business environments can best be characterized by change, complexity, constraints and conflicts; some observers go even further to mention chaos as an important environmental feature. Within this dynamic environment organizations have to ensure that they prosper, or at least survive." (D.J.W.Fender & D.Littlejohn, IJCHM, v4n3, 1992, p.i.)

The nature of managerial work means that the focus of attention generally lies within the organization. Yet, business uncertainty, caused by a turbulent and unpredictable environment, requires a broader perspective. An informed view of environmental influences and competitive forces is now an essential ingredient of strategic planning and development as managers need to be able to interpret events and detect trends quickly and accurately. To facilitate this, environmental scanning and impact analysis techniques can be used to assess the effects of economic, political, sociocultural, ecological and technological changes on the hospitality/tourism industries.

In this chapter:
- Arenas of economic change (F: 1 pp 8-16)
- The organization-environment interface (E: 1 pp 3-5; C: 8 pp 164-167)
- Environmental scanning (E: 1 pp 6-23 & H: 3 pp 41-69)
- Scanning systems and techniques (A: 3 pp 33-40; E: 1 pp 23-26; C: 8 pp 167-176)
- Modelling and forecasting (E: 1 pp 25-26; F: 12 & 13 pp 187-208)

REVIEW

Arenas of economic change (F: 1 pp 8-16)
The economic role and contribution of service industries has, during the 1980s and 90s reached the point whereby change affects the wider economic prosperity of Western nations. The mechanisms by which this occurs are complex and so service firms need to study an array of interacting market forces or arenas of change to determine the macro economic implications for their respective industries. The four principal arenas of change are: (a) financial or capital circulation; (b) material production and supply; (c) patterns of domestic consumption; (d) public service activities (see Figure 1.1 p.9).

The organization-environment interface
(E: 1 pp 3-5; C: 8 pp 164-167)
According to Daft (1) the external environment comprises all elements that exist outside the boundary of an organization and have the potential to affect all or part of its operations. In this context, environmental influences on international hospitality/tourism organizations are shown in Figure 1.1; different perspectives on the relationship between organizations and their environments in Table 1.1 (E: 1 pp 4-5).

The prosperity of an organization depends upon its ability to interact consistently and effectively with environmental variables. In its broadest sense, this is represented by an open systems model whereby resource inputs from the environment are converted into goods, services, information and waste by organizations and then released back into the environment (see C: 8 p.164). An effectively managed interface can be viewed in terms of: a quest for *homeostasis* (an ability to move forward in a more or less balanced way due to self-regulatory capabilities and a desire to maintain a steady state) and a quest to achieve *negative entropy* (effective responses to environmental change come from 'open' organizations, able to maintain momentum by importing the energy they need).

Emery and Trist (2) advocate the need for a wider view of organizational environments using a four-category classification model:

- *Placid-randomized environments* are characterized by limited change, predictable transactions and few, relatively passive change agents. This combination is comparatively easy to interpret. In these circumstances, organizations function most competitively as closed systems, focusing on optimizing internal efficiency.

- *Placid-clustered environments* comprise more powerful, active but well understood change agents. The rate of change is slow and change is predictable, providing an effort is made to monitor events.

- *Disturbed-reactive environments* are more complex and feature powerful, erratic change agents. Accordingly, the organization should seek to understand the interactive pattern of activity by closely monitoring events.

- *Turbulent fields* are environments in which powerful forces for organizational change develop in the firm's general environment, gather momentum and impact on the organization's task (or specific) environment. In such conditions, sophisticated monitoring procedures are needed to detect long-term developments and interconnectivity between environmental variables.

For many industries, the period from the mid-1980s to the early 1990s coincided with a rapid shift in environmental natures from the *placid-randomized* type to the *turbulent fields* type; a trend which has affected hospitality and tourism environments:

"...the existing complexity of the environment is expected to increase, as will variability and uncertainty...the hospitality manager must be capable of knowing and understanding the events which occur in his/her business and general environment." (M.D.Olsen, IJCHM, v1n2, 1989, p.3.).

Environmental scanning (E: 1 pp 6-23 & H: 3 pp 41-69)
Byars (3) defines environmental scanning as the systematic methods used by an organization to monitor and forecast those forces that are external to and not under the direct control of the organization or its industry. A list of definitions relating to the nature and process of environmental scanning can be found in Table 1.2; a review of contributions to the procedures and techniques used, in Tables 1.3 and 1.4 (p.6-10).

The *general* or external environment has many components (see Table 1.5, p.10), some of which interact or overlap. The key dimensions for scanning purposes are as follows:

Political dimension.
The political environment encompasses political systems, regulations and laws and, for firms trading internationally, an assessment of political stability and risk in host countries.

Economic dimension.
In general terms, economic prospects can be determined by reviewing a range of key indicators:
- *Gross National Product* (GNP) - a country's rate of growth and total annual market value of goods and services.
- *Income distribution* - the level of personal consumer income and consumption patterns.
- *Foreign exchange rates* - the rate of exchange of one currency for another; in Europe, the exchange rate mechanism (ERM) was designed to provide a benchmark and maintain stability.
- *Monetary and fiscal policies* (also exchange controls) - impose (a) limitations on the amount of money that can be taken out of the country and in some cases, (b) taxes on international transactions made by a foreign firm operating in a host country.
- *Financial and investment markets* - establish separate consumer and corporate interest rates, credit limits and availability and fluctuate according to prevailing rates of inflation, stock movements, share dealing and corporate reports.
- *Taxation and tariffs* - imposed by host country governments on individuals, corporations and imported goods.
- *Trade/industrial indicators* - provide overall measures of business activity which ultimately determine the state of the economy (prosperity, depression, recession, recovery).
- *Labour markets* - available skills, unemployment levels, re-training schemes and initiatives.

Sociocultural dimension.
Key components are *demographics* (profile attributes of consumers and the workforce); *culture* (patterns of behaviour shaped by factors including social class, family, subcultures, reference groups, lifestyle); *psychographics* (activities, interests, opinions, lifestyle, personality); *social factors* (relationships, attitudes, values, opinions, beliefs) *education*; *nationalism* (levels of patriotism).

Technological dimension.
Technology represents the utilization and application of available knowledge to improve production techniques and the technical specification of goods and services. Technological advancement, innovation and application to hospitality and tourism operations is notable in the areas of communication, transportation, safety and security, food and nutrition, computers, software and electronic equipment, robotics, energy, layout and design, equipment and packaging (see Table 1.6, p.17).

Ecological dimension.
Global ecological conditions, the availability of natural resources and other issues are of ever increasing significance to the hospitality/tourism industries. Areas of concern include: recycling, conservation, solid waste reduction, air quality, water quality and pesticides (see Table 1.7, p.19).

Operational dimension.
The operating environment has been variously described as the *task* or *specific* environment and

scanning activity focuses on five competitive forces; competitors, customers, suppliers and substitutes. Analysis of the specific environment enables the organization to identify its strengths and weaknesses, exploit opportunities and take action to minimize the impact of threats (see also chapter 6).

Scanning systems and techniques
(A: 3 pp 33-40; E: 1 pp 23-26; C: 8 pp 167-176)
A conceptual framework can help to determine the sequence and most appropriate set of scanning procedures for assessing the likely impact of environmental change on the organization (see for example Figure 3.4, A: 3 p.38.). To some extent, scanning activity is driven by the organization's overall information needs (see Figure 3.1, A: 3 p.35) and by critical or key success factors specifying focal concerns and courses of action in support of organizational goals or objectives. Figure 3.2 (A: 3 p.36) illustrates the kind of linkage that might be established between the organizational structure type, its objectives and related key success factors.

A progressive and selective filtering process is needed to identify and analyze information and to inform subsequent diagnosis and interpretation. Filters might include a review of:
- *sources* - reliable, consistent, accurate and valid information sources, closely linked to the organization's pre-determined key success factors.
- *actors* - individuals, institutions, organizations responsible for shaping change in their respective fields.
- *indicators* - changes in the activities and/or status of actors, which might in turn signify the need to review organizational objectives.
- *events* - evidence signifying the scope and direction of environmental changes taking place.
- *trends* - defined in terms of "...*a series of events which when grouped or clustered together point to a new or changing direction...In any given business environment there are several major and minor trends evolving at any given time which must be watched and evaluated in order to assess their impact on the firm.*" (M.D.Olsen, IJCHM, v1n2, 1989, p.4.)
- *scenarios* - to determine hypothetical situations and the possible courses of action to prevent, facilitate or solve likely outcomes.

There are a number of techniques that can be used in conjunction with environmental analysis. These include:
- Political, economic, social, technological (PEST) analysis - which can help the analyst to construct a general overview.
- Continuum models for classifying environmental natures (see Figures 8.3a; 8.3b C: 8, pp 168-169).
- Market attractiveness; product/market life cycle; Porter's five forces; opportunity/threat analysis.

Modelling and forecasting
(E: 1 pp 25-26; F: 12 & 13 pp 187-208)
A scanning system aims to capture and synthesize environmental data; the next step is to identify, predict and evaluate general and operating environment trends, threats and opportunities (see Table 1.9, E: 1 p.25). A range of qualitative and quantitative modelling and forecasting techniques can be used for this purpose:
- *Econometric modelling* - used to explore the relationships between economic and corporate activity using computer-aided regression analysis.
- *Trends analysis* - uses historical, seasonal, cyclical business statistics and general information to track and assess the likely impact of particular observed phenomena. This approach is routinely used by hospitality/tourism organizations and in so doing, it is necessary to address some of the limitations imposed by statistical sources. (For a discussion of tourism statistics see F: 12 pp 187-200.)
- *Probability forecasting* - seeks to determine likely outcomes from a given data set. (For a discussion of accuracy levels in probability forecasting for tourism see F: 13 pp 201-208).
- *Delphi technique* - uses expert panel views to construct a forecast of likely outcomes.
- *Scenario analysis* - involves the construction of two or more hypothetical situations which provide the basis for a subjective evaluation of possible courses of action to prevent, facilitate or solve a situation.
- *Brainstorming* - members of a group present forecasts based on individual judgment, knowledge and creative thinking. Concensus emerges from a discussion of plausible ideas and alternatives.

CONCLUSION

Hospitality/tourism organizations are confronted by a multitude of unpredictable and largely uncontrollable external forces which dictate the pace and nature of change:

"In surveying environmental changes which may affect organizations, managers have to distinguish between strong and weak movements. Essentially they are interested in identifying trends, which are increases or declines lasting long enough to bring

about a structural change or transformation of some activity or institution. These contrast against cyclical, temporary changes which leave untouched the basic conditions of society and its institutions, notwithstanding their short-term impact."
D.J.W.Fender & D.Litteljohn, IJCHM, v4n3, 1992, p.i.)

Environmental scanning and analysis provide a means of tracking events and detecting the emergence of trends so that structures and strategies can be adapted accordingly.

Review questions:

1. Comment on the economic impact of recession on the hospitality/tourism industries.

2. Identify and evaluate the potential impact of current trends in the general and specific environments on a hospitality/tourism organization of your choice.

3. Devise an information needs model for your placement organization/a firm with which you are familiar, and assuming no increase in the resource base, outline the environmental scanning procedures that might be implemented.

References:

1. R.L.Daft. *Organizational Theory and Design*. West Publishing, St. Paul, MN. 1989.
2. F.E.Emery & E.L.Trist. 'The Causal Texture of Organisational Environments', *Human Relations*, 18(1): 21-32, 1965.
3. L.L.Byars. *Strategic Management: Planning and Implementation; Concepts and Cases*. Harper & Row, New York, 1987.

EXTENSION

Read: Chapter 4 of *Managing Projects in Hospitality Organizations* (D: 4 pp 101-123).

The chapter addresses the role and future development of small and medium sized tourism enterprises (SMTEs) in the Aegean. It raises five key interrelated issues concerned with SMTEs, the impact of technology on destination marketing, the development of peripheral areas and islands, European Community relations and the need for an integrated strategic plan for the region. In particular, the chapter highlights a pressing need to evaluate sources of vulnerability (such as over-dependence on volatile, fashion-led markets) social and environmental impacts and a strategy to counter the threat posed by the growing influence and control of multinational companies.

Extension questions:

1. Evaluate the opportunities and threats for SMTEs arising from the Single European Act and comment upon the European Community's wider role in tourism development with particular reference to SMTEs and peripheral areas.

2. Discuss the key elements of a strategy which would assist SMTEs to compete more effectively at a tourist destination of your choice.

3. Assess the implications of new generation computerized reservation systems for the hospitality industry.

Practical exercises:

1. Choose an island destination, analyze the way in which its tourism industry is organized and review trends in tourism-related supply and demand. Using the framework in the chapter, undertake a SWOT analysis and by drawing on your findings, identify strategic options for the development of the island. Prepare a synopsis of your work for presentation and discussion.

2. Devise a model for quick internal and external business environment scanning appropriate to a small hotel business. Construct a tourism business network model which integrates the individual SMTEs in a destination of your choice. Draw up a list of the benefits arising from economies of scope, synergies and system gain to your small hotel.

3. Taking an island destination of your choice: (a) list the positive and negative impacts of tourism; (b) decide upon strategies to minimize the negative impacts; (c) assign the tasks necessary to achieve these strategies to individuals, businesses and agencies on the island; (d) simulate a public meeting run by the national tourist organization to raise these issues with students role playing the key roles of carriers, representatives of small businesses, representatives of inbound tour operators, environmentalists, local residents, local politicians and attractions owners; (e) summarize by reviewing the progress made and resolutions accepted by the group.

5 STRUCTURAL (INDUSTRY) ANALYSIS

INTRODUCTION

As noted in chapter 4, strategic analysis is the process by which an organization becomes better informed about its situation and its environment. This chapter will consider the nature of the industry in which a business operates and some of the key influences which impact upon it from both national and international perspectives.

Traditionally, managers have given most attention to the internal functions of the organization and to its efficiency. However, environmental change is accelerating and organizational success is now more closely related to the ability to adapt to largely uncontrollable events which shape national and international markets.

In this chapter:
- Porter's five forces (B: 24 pp 99-100; H: 7 pp 142-157)
- Generic competitive strategies (B: 24 pp 100-101)
- Changes in the UK hospitality market (A: 10 pp 163-165)
- Changes in international hospitality/tourism markets (E: 3 pp 38-63; A: 12 pp 194-212)
- Summary of global hospitality/tourism trends (E: Endword pp 346-351)

REVIEW

Porter's five forces (B: 24 pp 99-100; H: 7 pp 142-157)
The industry structure analysis approach to strategic management was proposed by Michael E. Porter of the Harvard Business School. He contends that competition in an industry is rooted in its underlying economics (1) and that profitability is affected by five major factors:

- *Rivalry.* The number and size of competitors will affect a company's profits through selling prices, as will the amount of growth in that industry.
- *Buyer power.* Buyers of products can influence the pricing or output of supplying firms under certain circumstances. If, however, the product represents a small purchase to the buyer or if it is differentiated from competing products, buyer power will not be so effective.
- *Supplier power.* Suppliers will be able to affect price and supply depending upon the number of suppliers, industry marketing methods, the availability of alternative sources of supply, or the degree to which the product is differentiated.
- *New entrants.* Barriers to entering an industry may consist of high capital costs, blocked distribution channels to customers, unfavourable government policy or high levels of existing customer loyalty and product differentiation.
- *Substitutes.* Should an industry be threatened with substitutes to their products, they will be unable to raise prices and profits because buyers would switch to the alternative products.

Generic competitive strategies (B: 24 pp 100-101)
Assuming that the impact on profitability of these five forces can been determined, one of three generic strategies can be deployed:

- *Pragmatic strategy.* The firm accepts the structure of the industry and seeks to reduce the impact of one of the forces by, for example, forming strategic alliances with a competitor.
- *Manipulative strategy.* In this strategy, the company tries to manipulate one of the forces by vertical or horizontal integration, or by acquiring a rival competitor.
- *Evolutionary strategy.* This strategy draws upon industry structural analysis to identify changes in the five forces, so that competitive advantage may be gained. For example, changes in government legislation relating to commercial food production may provide an opportunity for suppliers of refrigeration equipment to sell more of their products.

Having identified the forces at work and how they seem to be affecting the industry in general and specific component sectors, company strategists need to broaden their external analysis by assessing the implications for changes in demand from domestic and international markets. These are linked to key factors such as economic prospects, levels of employment, demographic changes relating to market segments, personal taxation and disposable income.

Changes in the UK hospitality market
(A: 10 pp 163-165)
Business travel both from within the UK and from abroad was a major source of revenue in Britain during the 1980s and is projected to grow in the 1990s, although at a slower rate.

The hypothesis of Kleinwort Benson's structural theory of business travel is that demand for business travel is determined by the structure of an economy rather than by growth in gross domestic product (GDP). It recognises three phases:
- *Phase 1.* Economies which experience minimal indigenous demand and which are characterized by reliance upon manufacturing and extractive industries. Despite the liberalization of trade in Eastern Europe, this scenario still prevails in Eastern bloc countries.

- *Phase 2.* As industries evolve from primary to secondary and tertiary sectors and as a greater number of multi-site companies develop, more domestic demand is generated for business travel. These conditions contributed to the rapid growth and high profits in the UK hotel sector during the early and mid 1980s.

- *Phase 3.* The third stage is perhaps best exemplified by the USA, where the service economy is at a mature stage of development and economic growth is marginal.

The high density of hotels in the UK compared with France, Germany and other parts of continental Europe combined with rapid development in other sectors of the UK hospitality industry contributed to the intensification of competition during the early 1990s. This, combined with *Phase 3* structural changes such as the errosion of UK manufacturing industry and the increasing reliance on services and especially tourism, requires a proactive management response.

Changes in international hospitality/tourism markets (E: 3 pp 38-63; A: 12 pp 194-212)
As noted above, the current general environment is characterized by change, complexity, constraints and conflicts. In response, managers must think strategically about the factors which shape trends in the international arena.
- *Government.* Within the international political dimension, a government's role is wide. It includes planning, regulation and influencing the economic climate through politics, legislation and economic development. Nevertheless, in some circumstances, government's role is brought into question by powerful multinational companies who exert pressure in order to influence policy on medium and long range development issues.
- *Demography.* Demography, the study of human population trends, affects industry demand (consumer markets) and supply (labour markets). Changes in the population and the age structure in turn, shape hospitality markets.
- *Social trends.* The current UK outlook is characterized by an increasing demand for travel, interest in health and cultural diversity. This is linked to the growth of two important groups of travellers; the 'young professionals' segment (age 25-44), who are single, well-travelled and educated and the 'grey market', comprising older consumers with a secure income, who are healthier and better educated than previous generations.
- *Economic and trading environment.* Growth in tourism is linked to economic development, that is the growth of GDP and per capita income. If government policy is non-interventionist, the relative influence of industry and commerce increases. To an extent, this was UK government policy during the 1980s and in such circumstances, multinational corporations are well placed to influence policy changes relating to the markets that they seek to serve.
- *Technological environment.* Technological advances in transportation (the development of the physical means by which passengers and goods are moved) and communications (telecommunications, computers, computer reservation systems) give rise to both opportunities and pressures to restructure so as to achieve productivity gains.
- *Internationalization of the hotel sector.* Historically, hotel sectors in the UK and elsewhere have been fragmented by size, dispersal and ownership of hotel units. The struture is changing however, as the number and size of multi-unit firms increased streadily during the late 1980s and early 1990s. The concept of an international hotel company has its origins in the late 1940s when American organizations began exporting branded American-style hotels to satisfy the needs of international travellers. This development partly reflected the dominant power of the US in world economic matters. In the mid-1960s international development was fuelled by the expansion of non-American hotel companies and in the early 1970s other sectors, notably fast food have sought to exploit overseas markets. The outcome of internationalization is an industry with a structure which is characterized by diversity, complexity, a multiplicity of ownership patterns is increasingly dependent upon successful product segmentation (or branding) strategies.
- *International hospitality organizations and the public policy chain.* In essence, the policy debate focuses on the extent to which governments should either encourage or regulate the development of multinational enterprises. While foreign investment may be encouraged,

the social and cultural traditions of the multinational enterprise may be very different to those experienced in the host community. International tourism is a complex field because of the multiplicity of factors involved and it requires the participation/collaboration of both governments and multinational agencies on tourism-related issues and policy formulation. Thus managers need a thorough understanding of the policy formulation process in order to understand the actions and motives of all participants and the obstacles that affect companies involved in tourism.

The countries in the Asia Pacific rim achieved strong economic growth in the 1980s *(Phase 2)* and they are striving to consolidate their position at the forefront of international tourism. However, such rapid growth has caused environmental, sociocultural and economic problems to the extent that hospitality/tourism organizations in the region are engaged in corporate diplomacy so as to play a more active role in solving the problems of mass tourism development.

Summary of global hospitality/tourism trends
(E: Endword pp 346-351)
Globally, the hospitality/tourism industries make a significant contribution to generating employment and GDP; likely patterns for the future are:

- *Changing industry structure*. The traditional independent family hospitality business is ill-equipped to meet the industry's mass demand and is likely to decline in significance. Coupled with this, multinational chains are expanding, often facilitated by strategic alliances (S.Crawford-Welch & E.Tse, IJCHM, v2 n1, 1990, pp 10-16). Consequently, there are likely to be fewer intermediaries and increased purchasing power in travel has increased the influence of those wielding a large volume business. (P.R.Gamble, IJCHM, v2 n1, 1990, pp 4-9.)

- *Investment*. During the 1970s and 1980s the hospitality industry and in particular, the hotel sector were viewed as secure, profitable capital investments. As property prices began to increase in line with inflation, higher returns were expected by shareholders. In the late 1980s, new ways were needed to manage strategic partnerships, particularly when building costs constrained new growth. Asset management became more important that asset holding. The 1990s has seen hotels closing and selling prices falling sharply and property price instability is set to continue.

- *Technology*. Consolidation has brought pressures for the industry to maximize its capacity, and technology can assist this process by facilitating improvements in performance monitoring, environmental scanning and customer service systems.

- *Pricing*. The era of consolidation and the greater concentration of buyer power have encouraged the development of sophisticated decision support systems (P.R.Gamble, IJCHM, v3 n4, 1991, pp 37-41) and the wider use of methods such as yield management to optimize capacity-pricing relationships (Pannell Kerr Forster Associates, IJCHM, v4 n2, 1992, pp i-iii).

- *Increasing activity in the political environment*. Widespread ecological concerns, the conservation movement and the growing influence of pressure groups such as Friends of the Earth and Greenpeace will cause politicians to re-draw the political agenda for the mid-1990s and beyond. Arising from this, the hospitality/tourism industries will have to take measures to improve current practices in relation to a wide range of environmental issues and in particular, waste water and solid waste management.

- *Firms are downsizing and decentralizing*. Global recession and intense pressure on profit margins arising from inflation, rising costs and competition, prompted much organizational restructuring in the late 1980s and early 1990s. This has meant that many hospitality/tourism organizations have fewer senior and middle management positions, reduced central support and specialist services and an enhanced role for unit managers (M.D.Olsen, IJCHM, v3 n4, 1991, pp 21-24).

CONCLUSION

During the 1980s, the UK hospitality industry experienced high levels of growth as the economy moved into *Phase 2* of the structural theory of business travel proposed by Kleinwort Benson. In contrast, the 1990s are likely to be characterized by the more difficult trading conditions of *Phase 3*, reinforcing the need for hospitality companies to become more:
- aware of the changing industry structure and emerging trends;
- perceptive with regard to developing products and services which match the prevailing trading conditions and circumstances;

- conscious of the impact of the international marketplace;
- flexible and pro-active in meeting consumer needs.

"Management, as a consequence, will need to become versatile, professionally trained and able to think strategically in a more hostile environment." M.D.Olsen, (E: Endword p 351).

References:

1. M.E.Porter, *Competitive Strategy: Techniques for Analyzing Industries and Competitors,* Free Press, New York, 1980.

Review questions:

1. What are Porter's five forces and what generic strategies are available to combat falling profitability? From your knowledge of a particular hospitality organization, report on how the relative importance of each of these factors affects corporate strategy.

2. Review the major changes affecting UK hospitality markets during the period from the mid-1980s to the present and, drawing from your evidence, forecast the foreseeable structural changes for the next ten years.

3. Identify the factors which affect change in international hospitality markets and identify how multinational companies might draw upon your interpretation to take advantage of prevailing conditions in both stable and turbulent overseas markets.

EXTENSION

Read: Chapter 2 of *Managing Projects in Hospitality Organizations* (D: 8 pp 33-76).

This chapter examines how Gloucestershire Services addressed the complex forward-planning issues associated with a period of rapid transition for school meals provision in the UK. It seeks to demonstrate that a detailed understanding of the consumer is fundamental to planning and management decision making in a changing environment and further, that all organizational activity is subject to the dynamics of its environment. In this, the chapter illustrates the value of a systems approach to managing organizations so that the full range of external and internal factors can be taken into account to ensure appropriate and effective planning.

Extension questions:

1. Investigate government policy on school meals from the 1970s to the present day. What do you think are, or will be, the social implications of this policy?

2. A number of commercial catering contractors have expressed the view that there is no scope for profit in the operation of school meals services. In the light of this view, discuss ways in which school meals could be provided without subsidy from local authorities.

3. Using the results of the Gloucestershire surveys of school feeding reported in the chapter, prepare a marketing and operational plan for Gloucestershire Services that addresses the longer-term stategic issues raised.

Practical exercises:

1. With reference to a sector of the hospitality/tourism industries with which you are familiar, identify the factors which have shaped its structure in recent years. Comments upon the trends which will affect its future development.

2. Define the terms 'internationalization' and 'globalization' and identify any perceived differences. How might these concepts affect the hospitality industry of the future?

3. What practical steps could organizations take to analyse industry trends and what benefits might they derive from doing so?

4. **Read:** D. Litteljohn & P. Slattery, *'Macro Analysis Techniques: An Appraisal of Europe's Main Hotel Markets'* IJCHM, v3 n4, 1991, pp 6-13. The authors contend that *"...competition in the European hotel market will be driven by two particular factors at a macro level. These are the nature of demand (opportunities) and the potential threats to profitability posed by prevailing levels of industry competition."* (p. 13). To what extend do you agree with this statement?

6 COMPETITOR ANALYSIS

INTRODUCTION

"In the '90s, the battle for market share will become an all-out war. This will be the most competitive decade in the history of the lodging industry. Every hotel and lodging company must become more market driven, improving their product, improving their service and examining their price in an effort to create a unique, sustainable, competitive advantage in the local marketplace and a perception of greater value for their guests." R.C.Hazard, Choice International (A: 5 p 72)

In a competitive world, companies need to continually examine strategies for achieving competitive advantage over their business rivals so as to stimulate growth of sales and profits. In hospitality and tourism, the key to competitive advantage is generally considered to be service excellence - that is providing a service which is perceived to be superior to that which is offered by rivals. Ultimately, if customers experience superior service, they are more willing to pay premium prices for the 'added value' of better service performance. In this regard, the competitive strategies used in the retail industry, where the concepts of branding and service superiority are well established, may be usefully analyzed by hospitality and tourism firms.

In this chapter:
- Competitive advantage (B: 28 & 29 pp 120-126)
- Generic marketing strategies (E: 6 pp 95-109; H: 8 pp 158-170)
- Standardization (A: 11 pp 175-176)
- Retail concepts and hospitality management (A: 6 pp 83-95)
- International marketing (A: 11 pp 166-193)
- Competitive international marketing strategies (E: 6 pp 95-109)
- Development strategies and ownership structures (E: 8 pp 126-132; A: 13 pp 221-224)
- Branding and franchising in the international hospitality industry (E: 5 pp 91-94; E: 7 pp 110-117; E: 13 pp 221-227)
- Developing a strategy for international operations (E: 8 pp 118-134)
- Globalization: future prospects (F: Summary pp 249-252)

REVIEW

Competitive advantage (B: 28 & 29 pp 120-126)
During the 1950s and 1960s, post-war consumer demand increased rapidly and the transition from product to market orientation began. The need for consumer-focused competitive strategy was reinforced by the falling rate of economic growth in the 1970s and in many markets, conditions of excess supply of goods and services. In conditions of intense rivalry between firms, it is in the best interests of a company to find a way of differentiating its product line so as to achieve the highest possible prices and levels of repeat business. This is termed differential advantage and is most commonly associated with superiority in aspects of product, service and supply.

Generic marketing strategies (E: 6 pp 95-109; H: 8 pp 158-170)
Miles and Snow (1) offer a strategic typology related to the degree of change that a firm is willing to accept:

- *Defender-like strategy.* The organization operates in a stable environment where emphasis is placed upon becoming as efficient as possible, protecting a specific segment of the market and offering a high quality product without risk at a competitive price. Reactions to environmental changes are defensive.
- *Prospector-like strategy.* Usually pursued by organizations operating in complex and dynamic markets where innovation is necessary in order to survive. Prospectors are constantly looking for new market niches by way of pro-active environmental scanning and consumer research activities.
- *Analyzer-like strategy.* A mixture of defender and prospector that attempts to minimize risk while maximizing the profit opportunity. It seeks to find new product markets while maintaining a strong customer base, by customizing the product.

These options are shown in figure 6.2 (A: 6 p 92).

Standardization (A: 11 pp 175-176)
Theodore Levitt argues that 'the world's preferences are becoming homogenized' (2) and manufacturing production-line methods should be applied to service industries. Crawford-Welch (A: 11 pp 175-181) suggests that the degree to which the marketing programme of an organization may be standardized depends upon:
- the target market
- market positioning

- the nature of the product
- the environment
- organizational factors

Retail concepts and hospitality management
(A: 6 pp 83-95)
"There is a degree of commonality between the hospitality and retail sectors. Both constitute large proportions of the service sector, employ large numbers of people and are essentially consumer-led." J.J.Lennon (A: 6 p 86)

The commonality of these two service industries offers scope for some interesting comparisons. The retail industry experienced considerable growth in the 1980s but is now characterized by intense price competition and smaller gross margins. Retailing is highly competitive, and aggressive marketing emphasizes consumer image and lifestyle. Branded retail outlets, like branded hotel chains compete for the attention and time of respective target markets.

Successful retailers have the flexibility to continually re-focus price, product and merchandising formats. This is a low-cost strategy which aims to present the uniqueness of the product, but this approach is relatively easy to imitate. Positioning strategy can be used to create a barrier to entry for imitative competitors, but it must be supported by a commitment to balance human resource needs in relation to the quality of service offered. In this sense, the most successful retail operators have combined improved customer care with enhanced productivity, utilizing technology to monitor stock control and record customer sales. Additionally, the retail industry has a good record of continuous innovation in support of competitive positioning and performance.

International marketing (A: 11 pp 166-193)
Instability in the domestic demand for hospitality services during the early 1990s is prompting more organizations to enter international markets. As competition increases, a growing number of hospitality companies are experimenting with more specific methods of market segmentation, that is, attempting to match their market orientation to the consumer behaviour of the target market. Further, the effectiveness of the marketing programme is dependent upon the ability to relate to the culturally diverse attitudes and values of overseas markets, thereby maximizing the impact of limited marketing resources.

Competitive international marketing strategies
(E: 6 pp 95-109)
In order to maximize competitive advantage in international markets, marketing strategy needs to evolve in relation to changing events. Accordingly, the traditional marketing mix, based on the 4Ps (product, place, price and promotion) may require adaptation; the aim being to anticipate market conditions rather than simply reacting to them. Key consideration are as follows:

- *Product*. Increased emphasis on customization and product branding.
- *Place*. Greater importance of indirect channels of distribution (such as consortia membership).
- *Price*. The traditional cost and discount pricing orientation may give way to customer-led pricing and yield management maximization.
- *Promotion*. Mass marketing may be replaced by micro-marketing and a stronger emphasis on green marketing. Internal marketing involves treating employees as internal customers who are seeking satisfaction from their contribution to meeting the objectives of the organization. Relationship marketing seeks to protect the customer base through the enhancement of customer relationships.

Development strategies and ownership structures
(E: 8 pp 126-132; A: 13 pp 221-224)
Typically, organizational expansion involves the development of one or more products by increasing geographical distribution, seeking forms of product improvement, utilizing penetration pricing, and expanding support networks. The most frequently used development strategies are:

- *Strategic alliance*. Strategic business units (such as hotels) may be linked via an independent central reservation and marketing system or a company may seek an overseas partner with local knowledge prior to entering a particular market.

- *Franchising*. A popular form of development in which the right to use a brand is licensed for one or more units to a franchisee.

- *Management contracts*. Firms with an established reputation for their management skills who seek to enter into contract to manage a property for one or more owners. In some cases, they also take an equity stake in the property; this is generally the policy adopted by Hyatt International Corporation.

- *Joint ventures*. This strategy is usually employed by a large real estate developer and a hospitality or travel-related firm. This strategy is different from the others, because it requires high capital investment, and therefore a higher level of risk.

- *Acquisition.* Acquisition has became a less desirable strategy for expansion, due to the high capital cost and long pay-back associated with purchasing property and other assets.

Branding and franchising in the international hospitality industry (E: 5 pp 91-94; E: 7 pp 110-117; E: 13 pp 221-227.)
The relationship between branding and franchising in the international hospitality industry is largely dependent upon the ability to replicate a distinctive service-product package in geographically diverse locations. Three different approaches to branding and expansion adopted by international hotel companies are outlined below.

- *Multibrand.* Choice Hotels International is one of the world's largest franchise hotel companies, and aims to be the global leader by the year 2000 with a projected 10,000 hotels. Choice have seven brands linked by one reservation system, and believe that this multibrand strategy offers the key to future success. They retain control of the product through quality specifications in franchise agreements and franchise holders are required to maintain the agreed product and service specifications.

- *Brand extension.* Holiday Inn Worldwide (HIW) have been using a brand extension strategy to rapidly expand their franchise operations in Europe. In this, effort is concentrated upon upon three hotel types in the mid-price to luxury lodging market. In order to protect the universality of the brand, as with Choice International, HIW specify design, construction and operating criteria in franchise agreements and regularly monitor standards.

- *Masterbrand.* In 1988, Hilton International carried out a major consumer audit which helped to reinforce a decision to develop 'service brands' such as 'Wa No Kutsurogi' (Japanese Service brand) which are endorsed by the Hilton International name. This and other service brands represent a comparatively new approach to hotel customization for specific markets based on country of origin and purpose of visit within the umbrella (or masterbrand) corporate identity of the company. Brand customization of this type is seen by Hilton as a effective response to developing services which meet culturally different needs. Hilton prefers not to franchise to other operators and in most cases, Hilton International properties are owned by investors and operated by Hilton International under a management contract.

Developing a strategy for international operations
(E: 8 pp 118-134)
In the past twenty years, advances in transportation and communication technologies have affected the nature of hospitality/tourism market competition. There are two generic categories for assessing sources and influences on the nature of competition:
- *Multidomestic.* Competition largely eminates from autonomous organizations operating within the host country.
- *Global.* The firm's competitive position in one country is influenced by its position in other countries. The firm must integrate its activities on a worldwide basis in order to maximize the gain derived from linkages among countries.

Motives for international expansion might be affected by the need to increase the levels of growth and profits, the increasing level of international travel and tourism or a search for protection from overdependence on one or more national economies by exploiting the differences in business cycles in host countries.

The hospitality industry has, during the 1990s, moved from a multidomestic orientation to a global perspective. Globalization is based upon a convergence in world tastes and product preferences, made possible by technology in communications and travel, and by the convergence of business practices in many countries. A global view requires a far more comprehensive review of international trends. Ultimately, a multinational business can only develop competitive advantage by optimizing efficiency and being willing to learn. It can however, benefit from economies of scale, it can exploit synergies and economies of scope and exploit cultural differences among many countries by using an appropriate mix of standardization and customization.

CONCLUSION

Globalization: Future prospects
(F: Summary pp 249-252)
Hospitality/tourism are global industries and the move to establish free-market economies in Eastern Europe and elsewhere will in time, increase the demand for hospitality and tourism services still further. Management strategists in service industries are concentrating their analyses upon the relationship and interaction between the firm, its employees and the customer. Service quality, as exemplified by the success of Japanese industry in the 1980s, is likely to remain a critical factor throughout the 1990s, but shortages in the supply of labour will not help organizations to maintain standards of service and

facilities. The challenge for firms seeking to protect their market share will be to make full use of the technological innovations which will enable them to keep in touch with the social, demographic and other forces shaping the nature of industry and market competition.

References:

1. R.E.Miles and C.C.Snow. *Organizational Strategy, Structure and Process,* McGraw Hill, New York, 1978.
2. T.Levitt, 'Production-Line Approach to Service' *Harvard Business Review,* September-October 1972, pp 41-52.

Review questions:

1. With reference to an organization with which you are familiar, analyze its marketing strategy using the typology proposed by Miles and Snow (1). Report and make recommendations as to suggested changes to that strategy and how they may be implemented.

2. What are the comparative advantages to hospitality/tourism organizations of:
a) strategic alliances; b) franchising;
c) management contracting; d) joint ventures;
e) acquisitions. In view of changing economic conditions, which are likely to be the most popular development strategies in the mid-1990s and beyond?

3. Review the forces which influenced internationalization during the 1970s and 1980s and speculate as to the future competitive strategy of multinational hospitality/tourism organizations.

EXTENSION

Read: Chapter 8 of *Managing Projects in Hospitality Organizations* (D: 8 pp 215-235).

The chapter is concerned with the Taj Group, who operate hotels of deluxe or five star standard internationally. Taj have developed their own methodology for systematically evaluating competitors, based upon the characteristics of good service leaders. The approach adopted by Taj may be regarded as commonsense, but it is vital to realize that what is obvious at a theoretical level must be understood and applied in practice.

Extension questions:

1. Companies such as McDonald's and Disney set very high standards although they are geared towards 'popular' markets. What can traditional deluxe hotels and restaurants learn from businesses such as these? What can the popular sector learn from 'up-market' operations?

2. Why is it that Asian companies have won many awards for excellent service? Are there links to culture or tradition, and can service excellence be learned or is it inherent?

3. Consider the systematic approach adopted by Taj in the light of a hotel with which you are familiar, and suggest any lessons which may be learned from them.

Practical exercises:

1. Prepare and deliver a presentation to 'sell' the idea of the Taj methodology to the senior management of a hospitality/tourism organization and include a strategy for its introduction to the company.

2. Consider the Cook Johnson research evidence detailed in Tables 1 to 17 in the Appendix to the chapter. Individually rank the 17 tables on the basis of which ones are the most important from the point of view of (a) the chief executive of an international hotel group concerned about creating competitive advantage based on service in his 'core' mid-market hotel brand (450 hotels in 46 countries) and (b) the manager of a 50 bedroom country house hotel aiming to achieve excellence in customer service. Aggregate the group rankings and produce a collective list of the five most important research findings. Consider your conclusions in relation to the *Zeithaml et al.* 5 gap model.

3. Setting service standards is one thing, training staff is another. Prepare a 'standards checklist' for use by supervisors and managers in the control of service standards in two of the following: a) Points of sale in a fast food restaurant; b) The reception desk in a deluxe resort complex; c) The service environment in a mid-priced family restaurant; d) A beach front ice cream and teas bar. Validate the checklists using role-play exercises and prepare a report on the exercise for plenary presentation.

7 PORTFOLIO ANALYSIS

INTRODUCTION

"The movement of a business organization across the decades, as it seeks to escape one increasingly hostile industry environment and relocate in a more benevolent one, can be likened to a journey of an interplanetary spaceship. Having made the decision to relocate and chosen the new base of operations, it takes enormous energy and thrust to escape the gravitational pull of the existing environment."
G.Donaldson & J.Lorsch. *Decision Making at the Top.* Basic Books, New York. 1983 p 173.

Portfolio analysis has been described as a methodology for generating a set of strategic options depending on the nature of the markets an organization is in and the organization's specific position within those markets (B: 22 p 88). It is mainly used by large organizations to assess the relative competitive position of each of its products and/or businesses. All companies need to analyze their organizational performance with reference to the external competitive environment and, case analysis can provide a specific vehicle from which appropriate strategy may be determined.

In this chapter:
- Boston Consulting Group (BCG) matrix (B: 22 pp 89-90)
- generic BCG strategies (B: 22 pp 90-91)
- General Electric matrix (B: 23 pp 93-94)
- Other portfolio analysis methods (B: 23 pp 94-97)
- Criticisms of portfolio analysis (B: 23 pp 95-96)
- Portfolio analysis for hospitality/tourism services (A: 6 pp 91-92)
- Strategic planning at Scott's Hotels
- Re-structuring the hotels portfolio at Forte PLC (E: 10 pp 163-170)
- Case analysis (C: 5 pp 92-114)

REVIEW

Boston Consulting Group (BCG) matrix (B: 22 pp 89-90)
The BCG matrix categorizes products and/or businesses according to relative market growth and market share (see B: 22 p 89, Figure 7) and proposes a four-part classification system:
- *Cash cows.* A strong market position in a declining market and therefore cash generators but with little growth potential.
- *Stars.* A strong growth position in an expanding market, but funding is needed to realize full potential.
- *Question marks.* Also referred to as a 'problem children' due to low market share in growth markets and the investment needed to support performance improvement.
- *Dogs.* Suffer the worst of both worlds; low market share in a declining market, while the expenses incurred in gaining business from competitors may not be cost-effective.

Generic BCG strategies (B: 22 pp 90-91)
The matrix offers four strategic options, each dependent upon the circumstances and situation of the product and/or business under review:
- *Build.* In a growing market, building offers the hope of future cash generation, but its success depends to some extent on the reaction of competitors; if they are complacent, it may be possible to gain market share, even in a declining market.
- *Harvest.* The strategy used to 'milk' a cash cow.
- *Hold.* The maintenance of market share and position using the resources generated by a cash cow.
- *Withdraw.* If market share/positioning is weak and prevailing conditions are static or projected growth is limited, the best option may be to divest and withdraw so as to concentrate resources on products/businesses in the portfolio with better prospects and potential.

Summarizing, the BCG matrix is often used by business strategists to structure thinking and planning. It lacks precision and predictive value, but as a descriptive tool it facilitates the mapping out of market positions and options across the product/business portfolio.

General Electric (GE) matrix (B: 23 pp 93-94)
The GE matrix also uses two axes; industry attractiveness and competitive positioning.
- *Industry attractiveness* is determined by: size of industry; profitability; growth rate; nature of competition; business cycle and ability to gain economies of scale.
- *Competitive positioning* is affected by: market share; profit level; management ability; production capability and technological strength.

Product/business portfolio positions on the GE matrix also depict relative sales turnover, using circles which correspond in size to the estimated share of total market sales turnover (B: 23 p 93, Figure 8). General Electric have successfully used the technique to increase profitability over a number of years by pioneering a policy of 'downsizing', that is, retaining only the most profitable companies in the corporate portfolio.

Other portfolio analysis methods (B: 23 pp 94-97)
Geographic analysis:
This matrix is often used to analyze the desirability of international expansion. In the example shown in Figure 9 (B: 23 p 94) country attractiveness is combined with business strength. Country attractiveness could include economic growth, political stability and market size, while business strength might embrace market share, profitability, distribution network, company image and the compatibility of the product to the culture of the host country.
Life-cycle analysis:
Using this matrix, the competitive position of a product or business is ranked on a scale from dominant to weak and plotted against its stage in the product life cycle. The four stages are: embryonic; growth; maturity and ageing. A range of generic strategies suited to each stage of development have been developed and one of more of these could be deployed, in accordance with positioning on the matrix.

Criticisms of portfolio analysis (B: 23 pp 95-96)
There are a number of criticisms associated with the prescriptive frameworks used in conjunction with portfolio analysis: they tend to be used in a mechanistic way; by relying on two main variables, others are ignored; the analysis is too subjective and simplistic to be of commercial value; the techniques are widely available, so strategies are open to imitation; they can discourage investment in products/businesses showing symptoms of failure; they are insensitive to the morale of managers deployed in declining businesses; they do not take account of future environmental impacts or unforeseen business potential.

Portfolio analysis for hospitality/tourism services
(A: 6 pp 91-92)
Effective competitive strategy for hospitality/tourism services should seek to exploit aspects of differential advantage. If a unique image is created in the mind of the consumer, the product may be difficult or expensive to imitate but due to the high incidence of imitation in hospitality/tourism, it is likely that 'brand champions' will emerge in the future. This development could be monitored using the matrix developed by McGee (1) which positions retail organizations in relation to cost and differentiation strategies. Figure 6.3 (A: 6 p 92) illustrates its application to the hotel sector. For instance, budget hotels are depicted as narrow-focus, cost-oriented operations while the 'luxury' hotel market offers broad-focus, differentiated products.

Strategic planning at Scott's Hotels
(IJCHM, v2 n3, 1990, pp iv-vi)
Scott's Hotels use a number of strategic models in support of their planning activities:
GE industry attractiveness matrix:
The model is used to determine which sector(s) offer the best investment opportunities and to compare the various alternative market segments that an individual hotel or the company as whole could focus upon. It is viewed as a useful summarizing tool that helps to facilitate a clear picture of the various segmentation options and the likely best option.
Ansoff matrix (see also chapter 10):
The model is used to review market objectives in accordance with a framework which offers four options; (a) existing markets/existing products; (b) existing markets/new products; (c) new market/existing products; (d) new market/new product. Uncertainty and risk increases as one moves into unfamiliar terrain and in this context, the model helps to assess corporate development strategies and to plan marketing activity for individual hotels. It also encourages logical questions such as: can we sell more to our existing customers? and can we develop new products for our existing market? These are key questions to address prior to taking existing products to new markets.
Porter's five forces/matrix of generic strategies:
An understanding of the five forces (see chapter 5) facilitates a systematic review of competitive positioning from the perspective of the company and the individual hotels. It is also important to determine whether to be a low-cost producer, selling at the lowest price (or making the highest margin) or to be differentiated in some product attribute(s) highly valued by the customer, thereby attracting a premium price.
Gap Analysis:
Sub-divided into profit and market gaps; each linked to an exploration of the causes and solutions.

Re-structuring the hotels portfolio at Forte PLC
(E: 10 pp 163-170)
Forte recognized in the late 1980s that a corporate re-branding strategy was needed to combat rival companies who were operating better focused hotel brands and threatening Forte's market share. It was decided to link the name Forte with the brand name, unifying the separate hotel brand types and collections in the portfolio, each targeted to meet the needs of specific market segments.

Newer and purpose-built hotels were allocated to one of three brand types: *Forte Travelodge* offering roadside budget accommodation; *Forte Posthouse* modern hotels and competitive prices; *Forte Crest* business hotels specializing in personal recognition and service.

The older Forte properties were allocated to one of three collections: *Forte Heritage* traditional British inns combining comfort, service and character; *Forte Grand* first-class hotels offering traditional European standards of comfort, style and service; *Forte Exclusive* a collection of internationally renowned hotels offering the finest standards of comfort, style and service.

The process began by re-defining the brand structure so as to clearly determine what each brand would offer in relation to differences and commonalities across the hotels portfolio. Employees were made aware of the reasons for the re-branding and fully briefed about the process of organizational change that occurred. The overall communications strategy successfully minimized the sense of ambiguity and anxiety which accompany change, set out simpler, more effective operational policies and procedures and raised awareness of the company's strategic aims for the 1990s, which are: to enable the group to fully exploit its collective strengths; to establish a clear position in expanding international markets; to develop a common purpose by identifying more closely with core businesses; to create opportunities for cross-selling, effective marketing and increased profitability.

In common with hotel-led international expansion, the rationalization of the group is likely to continue, with the possibility of further product portfolio divestment so as to maintain clarity of direction and focus.

Case analysis (C: 5 pp 92-114)
Case analysis can offer a realistic way of appraising business performance as it provides a mechanism for integrating information about the company's history, internal operations and external environment. Each situation is unique, and requires careful diagnosis and evaluation through the application of theoretical knowledge and an understanding of management practice.

Case analysis requires a sequential and systematic approach which involves: examining and identifying business situations (problems, opportunities); researching possible causes; generating alternatives and feasible courses of action; formulating and implementing strategy. At each stage, appropriate matrices may be used to assist with the analysis.

The use of matrices during the preliminary stages of the analysis helps with the identification of strengths, weaknesses, opportunity and threats (SWOT analysis), a common starting point for deeper analysis and causal investigation. Strengths (and weaknesses) are attributes of an organization which provide an advantage (or disadvantage) over other organizations, especially competitors, while opportunities and threats are external to the company. An opportunity represents a prospect for adopting a new or revised strategy that could be of benefit to the organization. Threats constitute possible events which may seriously hamper an organization's ability to achieve its mission, or even threaten its entire existence.

To ensure that the case is relevant and meaningful, it should include an analysis of the organization's competitors and operating environments (general, economic, industry, sector). This facilitates scenario building by providing much of the business picture surrounding past, present and foreseeable events.

Financial data provides a further dimension of analysis and to facilititate the interpretation of figures, summary statistics and ratios should be calculated. A typical financial analysis would include the identification of trends in sales, profits and cost ratios. Further, there should be a comparison of these to industry norms and averages.

The identification of the firm's mission is of vital importance to the whole of the decision process and the organizational structure should be analyzed to assess whether the structure (centralized or decentralized) fits the internal and external environments. It is also important to assess the performance of senior management, styles of management, communication and interrelationships between management and employees.

CONCLUSION

The effectiveness of strategy depends to some extent, upon an accurate assessment of where the organization is positioned compared to its rivals. In a dynamic and changing external environment, large organizations must ensure that every type of operation within their corporate portfolios is operating to best effect. Strategies to maximize performance can benefit from the use of portfolio analysis, despite its predictive limitations. However, Porter (2) notes that portfolio planning tools may obscure the most essential strategic issue in constructing a firm's portfolio of business - the creation and enhancement of interrelationships.

In dealing with this issue, businesses of any size can benefit from undertaking a case analysis of their internal operations and external environment. If correctly applied, the methodological discipline involved invariably yields insights on the many different forms of interrelationships which can greatly assist the process of strategic planning and development.

References:

1. J.McGee. Retail Strategies in the UK, in Johnson G., (Ed) *Business Strategies and Retailing,* John Wiley, Chichester, 1987.
2. M.Porter. *Competitive Advantage: Creating and Sustaining Superior Performance.* Free Press, New York, 1985 p 381.

Review questions:

1. Describe each of the four categories in the Boston Consulting Group matrix, and justify the selection of examples for each category drawn from the hospitality/tourism industries.

2. Write short notes on the characteristics of the General Electric matrix and suggest other matrices which may be appropriate to service industries.

3. Review the steps associated with the preparation and analysis of a business case study and comment upon the benefits and limitations of this approach.

EXTENSION

Read: chapter 10 of *Managing Projects in Hospitality Organizations* (D: 10 pp 263-289)

This chapter focuses on some of the ways in which one large chain in the fast food sector coped with changes in the traditional labour market brought about by a period of demographic change. The project used case analysis to generate some interesting questions for Burger King concerning age preferences in employment and the problems of matching staff-customer age, sex and cultural profiles. In addressing these issues, Burger King were also seeking a better product-market fit by endeavouring to ensure that unit staffing policy mirrors the demographic and cultural profile of the unit catchment area.

Extension questions:

1. Identify the most common stereotypes associated with a person's age and the assumptions which are often associated with stereotyping. If you were the manager of a fast food restaurant how would you tackle these issues in your dealings with staff?

2. Should the strategy for the development and implementation of a changed employee profile be decided in the boardroom, leaving implementation to lower managerial levels, or should a board of directors focus on the company's mission statement, leaving both strategy and implementation to the company's operational managers?

3. To what extent should companies in the fast food sector be pro-active in relation to problems of demographic change and to what extent can they afford to be reactive? Now that the predicted shortage of younger employees may not arise, should human resource strategies at Burger King be modified, and how?

Practical exercises:

1. Analyze a large hospitality/tourism organization using portfolio analysis to determine the medium term prospects of its products and/or component businesses and comment upon the organizational implications using appropriate criteria to justify your views on the issues facing the organization as a whole.

2. Choose a service industries case study and undertake a detailed functional analysis of a) finance; b) marketing; c) human resources; d) operations. In the presence of an impartial observer, formally discuss the strategic issues which arise and try to determine an overall strategy. On completion, discuss the process of decision-making with the observer and highlight areas of perceived weakness.

3. A large multi-unit company has invited your hospitality and tourism consultancy group to give a presentation on the benefits and disadvantages of portfolio analysis, with particular reference to its role in facilitating internal analysis. Select different group members to advance the proposition and to criticise it and finally invite the audience (board members) to vote on its adoption by the organization.

8
OPERATIONS ANALYSIS

INTRODUCTION

"...it would be pointless to try to run hotels in the same way as independent owner/operators. It is more sensible to ensure that the various divisions develop a unique form of competitive advantage derived from the company's size and specialist expertise. In this way the business can be geared towards performance standards which it can replicate easily and effectively." Rocco Forte (A: 1 p.7)

Decision-making in the operational sphere centres on the deployment of resources in order to achieve pre-determined objectives. It demands an ability to balance the need for profit optimization against the necessary investment required to meet quality standards and satisfy customers consistently. The dynamic nature of the customer interface means that managers must continually seek feedback on operational performance so that variances can be identified and improvements made. To facilitate this, managers need to establish an appropriate framework for sampling, auditing and refining the operations environment.

In this chapter:
- Systems design (A: 3 pp 34-37; E: 18 pp 317-319; E: 15 pp 255-273)
- Improving quality (A: 5 pp 72-82; A: 8 pp 120-143; A: 9 pp 151-157; E: 18 pp 312-318)
- Improving productivity (F: 6 pp 92-109)
- Improving profitability
- Assuring operational standards (D: 6 pp 205-209)

REVIEW

Systems design (A: 3 pp 34-37; E: 18 pp 317-319; E: 15 pp 255-273)
Accurate, timely information is essential to the design and management of hospitality/tourism operations. The assessment of information needs should, ideally, form part of an integrated plan for both internal and external operating environments (see for example, A: 3 p.35).

In this way, evidence of change in the external environment helps to inform decision-making about the need for operational change and the related implications for product and service specification.

Internally, the accuracy and reliability of a management information system depends on the design concept, the technology used and the nature of the human interface that it provides. In theory, information technology is capable of providing wide ranging operational support, providing that certain endemic limitations are dealt with:

- *span* - the perspective must change from a nine/twelve month time horizon to a much longer period.
- *staffing* - personal productivity in service industries is low. A new emphasis on productivity and performance is needed in which a more technical orientation to jobs and to personal development is created. The skills base needs to shift away from a product orientation to a managerial and service orientation.
- *service* - service quality is closely linked to standards of staffing. A low-paid, poorly-trained staff are unlikely to be able to maintain service quality.
- *organizational structure* - should be opinion seeking and less autocratic; information technology can play a key co-ordinating role in facilitating a change of managerial style.
- *systems* - should concentrate on outputs and not on the detail of control over inputs. The industry has a tendency to over-control and lose sight of what is really important.(P.R.Gamble, IJCHM, v3n1, 1991, pp 15-16.).

The principal concern of service design is to specify the elements and interactions for a given service. This is inseparably linked to notions of cost, product and consumer orientation (see chapter 9) revenue and rate of return decisions and the interpretation and emphasis placed on three key concepts - quality, productivity and profitability:

quality - emphasizes the optimization of customer satisfaction by adding value to the product-service package, generating repeat business and building revenue.

productivity - places emphasis on maximizing resource effectiveness by manipulating product-service inputs to achieve desired outputs.

profitability is a measure of financial performance which can be enhanced by seeking the optimum balance between capital employed, cost inputs and revenue generated.

These concepts are inter-linked and simultaneous improvement in all three areas can be achieved by adopting a flexible and pro-active operations strategy:

"Systems development is an ongoing process and it is easy to be diverted by technical innovations which may or may note prove useful in managing operations more efficiently...the focus of activity is on improving design specifications in facility construction, equipment specification and systems implementation rather than on devising new design concepts. By concentrating on improving or updating aspects of design, it is also possible to make progress in achieving higher quality standards and greater operational efficiency." Rocco Forte (A: 1 p.6)

Improving quality (A: 5 pp 72-82; A: 8 pp 120-143; A: 9 pp 151-157; E: 18 pp 312-318)
In order fully to address quality issues, hospitality/tourism organizations need to identify and devise ways of dealing with the complex combination of product/service tangibles and intangibles. To some extent, the need for quality improvement is driven by:
- *consumer expectations* - as determined by pricing, positioning, market and consumer profiles and the relative strengths and weaknesses of competitors;
- *technological innovation* - the pace of change and the cost of adding value to the product specification by adopting innovative features;
- *competitive positioning* - service excellence is increasingly viewed as a key factor in attaining differential advantage in domestic and international markets.

The aim of a quality improvement programme should be to attain 'right first time, every time' status for all resource inputs. Crosby (1) estimates that service firms waste as much as 35 percent of production costs on 'non-quality' performance. He advocates greater emphasis on prevention to reduce the 'cost of quality' associated with:
- *costs of failure* - arising from mistakes;
- *costs of appraisal* - associated with inspection routines to reduce the frequency of mistakes;
- *costs of prevention* - apportioned to training staff and improvements to the service delivery system designed to reduce errors and inconsistencies.

Above all, quality improvement requires a sustained effort to empathize with the customer and to respond accordingly. Improvements to the service delivery system can only be achieved by identifying the 'fail points' from the customer's perspective and by exploring how customers feel and react during service delivery. In hotels, customers enter a long and complex service delivery system characterized by many different types of interaction with other customers, service personnel, the operational environment and service systems. Inevitably, customers assess and evaluate the cumulative impact of successive interactions and experiences according to how they feel and whether the outcome was satisfactory or not. This raises a number of implications for the way in which quality improvement needs are identified. A systematic approach might include:
- *a customer audit* - to identify design impacts (such as reactions to design features, atmospheric effects and sources of irritation with service system design) and to assess the overall level of customer-focus;
- *an appraisal of front-line personnel* - to determine how well staff cope with operational pressures, levels of sensitivity to individual customer needs and to receive suggestions and new ideas from the staff responsible for delivering service;
- *a review of systems support* - to assess the adequacy of systems and procedures and whether they are consistently easy-to-use without delays or breakdowns;
- *action to minimize sources of customer dissatisfaction* - to ensure that lines of communication and decision-making facilitate the detection of and rapid response to service problems.

Improving productivity (F: 6 pp 92-109)
"The service sector has been blamed for reducing national productivity, and in particular the hotel sector has been seen to be a particularly poor performer. Difficulties of definition and measurement of productivity do exist, but this should not be used as an excuse for poor productivity in hotels and the service sector generally." (C.Witt and S.Witt, IJCHM, v1n2, 1989, p.33)

Armistead cites three key factors which act as barriers to quality improvement:
- *Specification of quality standards* is often difficult due to the intangible nature of services and the variability of customer expectations.

- *Control systems* rarely include statements defining what is to be measured, what the targets are, how measurements are to be made and by whom.

- *Staff development* often fails to make staff aware of quality objectives and fails to provide them with the capability to meet targets.

The *specification, control* and *development* issues also impede efforts to achieve improvements in productivity arising from:
- failure to understand the needs of the customer;
- failure to understand what really happens in the service delivery process;
- confusion in the flow of information, materials and people in the service process;
- lack of understanding between different stages in a service delivery system;
- unplanned changes in the way the service is produced and delivered;
- poor quality of service;
- failure to measure productivity;
- failure to measure the right things, i.e. those which are directly linked to the aspect of productivity that is most important: input costs, efficiency or utilization;
- reliance on a single productivity measurement;
- use of measures which are too complicated and discrete values rather than trends.

This analysis yields several key implications for managers seeking to improve service quality and productivity:
- quality and productivity should be linked to customer needs and expectations;
- quality and productivity should be linked to corporate objectives, i.e. decisions on service levels should take account of cost implications;
- productivity and quality have no absolute measures and so measurements should reinforce critical aspects of customer service;
- productivity and quality improvement require the support and understanding of all staff.

Improving profitability
Harris (2) asserts that effective operational profit planning requires a knowledge of:
- technical and business activities relating to the market, operations and employee policies;
- cost-volume-profit (CVP) analysis and the limitations of its underlying assumptions;
- computer spreadsheet operation and design.

The CVP technique facilitates the identification of break-even sales volume - an important intermediate target to be attained prior to making a profit. It assumes knowledge of the revenue and cost behaviour for a given operation and if this condition is met, it provides a mechanism for testing the profit potential of different business options. (P.J.Harris, IJCHM, v4n4, 1992, pp 24-32.)

Pannell Kerr Forster Associates (PKFA) sought to explain hotel profit differentials by investigating the interrelationships between operating efficiency, marketing, delivery of service and product specification (PKFA, IJCHM, v4n2, 1992, pp i-ii.). They were intrigued to know why two similar hotels operating in the same market, with comparable profits and locations, performed at different levels of profitability. To investigate further, they selected ten pairs of hotels in ten different European cities and compared levels of profit performance. Each of these pairs of hotels were comparable in terms of size, quality, tariff levels and the market in which they operated. The more profitable hotel of each pair was included in Group A, the less profitable in Group B and the resulted were analyzed in aggregate form. This approach uncovered dramatic differences in profitability between the two groups, a finding which appears to be closely linked to operational practices.

Key recommendations for improving profitability relate to:
- *productivity* - involve employees in the control of costs and profit planning;
- *performance* - management from department heads upwards should be fully involved in budget preparation, variance analysis, decision-making and guest service reviews;
- *payroll control* - the largest single controllable cost in any hotel operation with a disproportionate impact on profitability. Seek to maintain the most appropriate balance of full-time and part-time staff;
- *cost control* - apply techniques such as zero-based budgeting and periodically review controls for purchasing, receiving, storing and issuing.

PKFA conclude that: *"...the attainment of higher revenues is a far greater contributor to movements in profit than cost control. We believe that service is the attribute which contributes most to secure this additional revenue, with marketing an important, but subsidiary factor."*

CONCLUSION

"During the past five years a much clearer model has emerged for quality management in hospitality systems. This is particularly the case for the variously termed intangible, functional or 'service' aspect of the hospitality product. Here there is a concensus that total commitment by management, employee ownership and empowerment and a strong sense of mission are vital ingredients..."
N. Johns (IJCHM, v5n1, 1993, p.14.)

Assuring operational standards (D: 6 pp 205-209)
The interrelationships between quality, productivity and profit performance clearly demonstrate the need for a systematic approach to operational planning

and analysis. Systems for managing quality in manufacturing have existed for a long time; more recently hospitality/tourism organizations have sought to apply a similar discipline to assuring operational consistency in a services context. British Standards Institute accreditation (BS 5750) provides an increasingly popular route to attaining this goal.

BS 5750 represents an operating philosophy for goods and services; it requires the preparation of a quality manual specifying systems and procedures covering every aspect of the operation (S. Counsell, IJCHM, v3n3, 1991, pp iii-iv.). The aim is to ensure that operating standards are consistently achieved in accordance with performance targets for every facet of a hospitality/tourism operation. Further, a pro-active approach is encouraged by establishing procedures for corrective action, continual improvement and quality auditing (3). In some cases, the attainment of BS 5750 represents an important step towards implanting a total quality culture (see chapter 15) - arguably, the most significant organizational challenge for the 1990s.

Review questions:

1. Identify and discuss the differences of approach needed to audit service delivery systems in owner-operated small businesses and large, multidivisional companies, each with its own distinctive product portfolio.

2. Investigate the reasons why productivity in service businesses is generally lower than in manufacturing. How should hospitality/tourism businesses address this problem?

3. Evaluate the impact of operational policies and procedures on profit performance in an operation of your choice.

References:

1. P.Crosby. *Quality is Free,* McGraw-Hill, New York, 1979.
2. P.J.Harris. *Profit Planning,* Butterworth-Heinemann, Oxford, 1992.
3. Hotel, Catering & Institutional Management Association, *Managing Quality,* 1993.

EXTENSION

Read: Chapter 7 of *Managing Projects in Hospitality Organizations* (D: 4 pp 169-213).

The chapter addresses the Sutcliffe Catering Group's strategic quality management initiative and the operational implications of BS 5750 accreditation. This is set in the context of intense rivalry among contract catering firms, all seeking to secure competitive advantage from quality improvement and assurance.

Extension questions:

1. Identify the information needs and outline the data collection methods which you would recommend to a contract catering company wishing to fully audit its quality standards. Recommendations should take into account the differing perspectives of (a) clients (b) customers (c) managers and supervisors employed by the contractor (d) operatives working for the contractor.

2. Profile the ideal behavioural characteristics of 'front-line' staff in a contract catering environment and outline the management action needed to attain these ideals in the context of a quality improvement programme.

3. Identify and evaluate the potential value of BS 5750 accreditation to firms operating in the following sectors (a) fast-food; (b) roadside restaurants; (c) hotels serving mainly business markets.

Practical exercises:

1. Conduct a survey in a hospitality/tourism unit of your choice, with the aim of identifying perceptual differences on the issue of quality. The survey should involve management, supervisors, operatives and customers. Use the 'SERVQUAL' dimensions (D: 6 p.176) as the basis for your investigation.

2. Design a checklist for a quality audit, which should be conducted in an operation of your choice. The checklist should be capable of generating clear evidence as to whether quality management procedures are effective.

3. Conduct an assessment of the quality costs of a selected company and design a 'quality consciousness' programme to reduce these costs. Forecast the likely reactions to your proposals and outline how the programme should be implemented and monitored.

9 RESOURCE ANALYSIS

INTRODUCTION

A prerequisite of business success is the ability to make the best use of all of the resources which are available to an organization. If the economic and social environment becomes more dynamic, resources must be managed more intelligently and sensitively if the organization is to maintain its position. In order to optimize resource deployment, it is necessary to establish effective monitoring methods which act as 'early warning systems' and, instil an on-going and questioning attitude towards performance improvement.

In this chapter:
- Maximizing activities in the value chain (B: 25 pp 102-106)
- Productivity (A: 4 pp 45-48 & E: 16 pp 275-295)
- Performance appraisal using financial methods (A: 4 pp 49-52 & E: 16 pp 275-295)
- Labour productivity (A: 4 pp 55- 71)
- Productivity strategies (A: 4 pp 59-65)
- Human resource implications (A: 7 pp 97-119)
- Human resource management strategies (A: 7 pp 99-119 & E: 17 pp 296-311)
- Productivity in Japan (B: 43 pp 178-199)
- Resource strategies for the 1990s (A: 4 pp 65-69)

REVIEW

Maximizing activities in the value chain
(B: 25 pp 102-106)
Porter's value chain (1) separates the activities of a business organization into primary and support activities. Primary activities include:
- *Inbound logistics* receiving, storing and handling inputs;
- *Operations* converting inputs to final product;
- *Outbound logistics* distributing the product to the customer;
- *Marketing and sales* communication with the customer;
- *Service* activities which enhance the value of the product.

Support activities comprise:

- *Procurement* the process for acquiring inputs;
- *Technology development* improving the process or product;
- *Human resource management* recruiting, training, developing and rewarding members of the organization;
- *Management systems* control systems for planning and finance.

The management of activities in the value chain can be assessed using two different but complimentary measures; efficiency and effectiveness:
- *Efficiency* is an evaluation of how well resources have been utilized, irrespective of the purpose for which they are deployed (2). It is concerned with the ratio of outputs from the value chain to inputs, and measures of efficiency might include profitability, yield and capacity.
- *Effectiveness* measures the deployment of resources with regard to the organization's stated aims and objectives. The relative degree of effectiveness therefore depends upon the fit between projected and actual outputs and on management's success in developing harmony and synergy throughout the value chain.

Productivity (A: 4 pp 45-48 & E: 16 pp 275-295)
Productivity is measured by considering the relationships between wealth generated and resources used to achieve a given volume and quality standard. A key question for management is whether to adopt a cost, product or consumer productivity orientation:
- *Cost orientation* is most suited to competitive trading conditions, such as a prevailing surplus of supply. Cost of sales related outputs provide a yardstick against which an organization's efficiency can be measured.
- *Product orientation* is a strategy aimed at achieving high profits by maximizing sales when demand conditions are favourable.
- *Consumer orientation* is a marketing-based strategy directed at maximizing customer satisfaction, which, in conditions of market decline, may provide a source of competitive advantage.

Performance appraisal using financial methods
(A: 4 pp 49-52.& E: 16 pp 275-295)
Growth in hospitality and tourism worldwide accelerated rapidly during the late 1980s but the recession of the early 1990s has caused a significant number of business failures. The level of capital investment required to finance new development often culminates in high fixed operating costs and a long pay-back period. Further, operating costs can escalate rapidly, so techniques which provide the basis of an 'early warning system' are valuable.

Business failure is commonly linked to one or more of the following factors: insufficient profits; high interest rates; loss of market share; reductions in consumer spending; lack of managerial expertise and experience; loss of key management personnel; inadequate sales due to economic decline; competitive weaknesses; poor location(s); heavy operating expenses; costly expansion programmes; loss of corporate direction.

The most commonly used technique for predicting business failure is ratio analysis, sometimes called univariate analysis, which is based on the calculation of individual ratios using data from the company's trading accounts and balance sheet. Accounting ratios provide a valuable measure of an organization's overall viability and their predictive power is derived from calculating and comparing the same ratios over a period of time in order to establish whether the business situation is stable, improving or declining. Further, by comparing ratios between similar businesses, it is possible to see whether the company is performing better or worse than the average (or norm) for the sector and the industry as a whole.

Some writers argue that traditional ratio analysis is not a reliable monitoring device because it fails to take account of changes in the business environment and that businesses have continued to fail despite their use. To counter this criticism, multidiscriminant analysis, which is a technique which combines several traditional ratios to produce a weighted statistic, can be used to assist in measuring comparative productivity and performance more scientifically.

To monitor performance at departmental level, ratios may be expressed in two ways:
- *Revenue ratios* measure sales against budgeted sales. Operating department measures of performance for a hotel rooms division would typically include: occupancy percentage; guest, sleeper or bed occupancies; maximum apartment revenue; average room rate; average spend and room occupancy percentage. Revenue ratios used in food and beverage operations include restaurant occupancy; average spending power; sales revenue per employee and the percentage of food to beverage or rooms.
- *Cost ratios* are primarily used to measure actual costs relative to past performance, and as such, they are useful to management in assessing business efficiency. Hospitality/tourism organizations use gross profit and net margin ratios to monitor overall cost profit relationships and this facilitates the development of performance benchmarks, especially in food and beverage areas.(A: 4 p 54).

Labour productivity (A: 4 pp 55-71)
Service industries need to ensure that their activities at the margin of the value chain enhance the value of the product, and labour is a resource which is crucial to productivity. However, labour often constitutes the most expense operating item to a hospitality/tourism enterprise and it is a resource which must be managed according to fluctuations in demand levels. In practice, one of the most difficult tasks of the unit general manager is to maximize labour efficiency while ensuring that quality standards are maintained.

Productivity strategies (A: 4 pp 59-65)
There are two generic strategies which can be applied to increase productivity:
- *Expansive.* Greater market share or product quality is sought through increased marketing efforts while resource inputs are maintained.
- *Contractive.* This strategy is a cost-orientated one in which volume and quality levels are sustained while resources are decreased.

Hospitality/tourism organizations seeking to expand their operations are more likely to adopt an expansive productivity strategy, but contractive strategies may assist cost reduction in materials, physical plant, energy, labour and general overhead costs, as follows:
- *Materials.* Food and beverage departments can reduce the cost of materials by controlling wastage and pilferage or by purchasing cheaper or alternative materials. Re-specification of the product can also lessen material cost, as can the achievement of economies of scale in larger organizations.
- *Physical plant.* Accommodation services provide a major source of income, so productivity savings must be balanced against customer and organizational expectations of quality standards for physical amenities and facilities.
- *Energy.* Recent advances in technology have led to the design of more economical equipment and automated control of energy costs.
- *Labour.* Costs may be minimized by reducing staffing levels or rates of pay, but this strategy may undermine staff morale and thus affect customer service. Hospitality/tourism organizations may have much to learn from the application of productivity techniques in manufacturing. Production line operations are routinely scrutinized so that improvements can be identified and implemented by re-organizing facilities, improving scheduling and involving

employees in the improvement process or by making better use of manufacturing technology.

Authors differ on the relative merits of expansive and contractive strategies, but all agree that service is the key ingredient in improving product intangibles, and that such productivity improvements can only be made through people working in the organization.

Human resource implications (A: 7 pp 97-119)
Managers working in hospitality/tourism organizations should always be aware of how change agents are affecting the human resource supply. These include:
- *Population changes.* Growth in the service sector of the economy combined with demographic changes will inevitably result in fewer young people being available for employment in the UK. Increasingly, organizations like Burger King (D: 10 pp 263-289) are exploring alternative sources of labour and alternative methods of work scheduling so that older workers and more specifically, women with young families can undertake flexible working, job sharing or fractional full-time roles.
- *Single European market.* It is anticipated that demand generated from within the European Community will create more jobs and promote labour mobility.
- *New technology.* Service industries such as banks have increased productivity and enhanced the range and speed of services they provide by adopting advanced technology. To a lesser extent, central reservation systems have improved global communications in the hospitality/tourism industries, but there are many working practices which have yet to harness the potential benefits of technological innovation.

Human resource management strategies
(A: 7 pp 99-119 & E: 17 pp 296-311)
Given the nature of labour market changes which are occurring, the advances in technology that are taking place and the need for continuous innovation in guest services, human resource managers need to draw upon an array of generic labour strategies in accordance with organizational needs. These include:
- *restructuring* - to facilitate organizational change;
- *technology-driven* - involving skills training and/or reductions in staffing levels;
- *procedural changes* - involving new or revised systems and procedures and consequent staff training;
- *substantive changes* - such as new agreements on aspects of pay and conditions;
- *behavioural changes* - designed to implant different work attitudes and behaviours.

It is anticipated that future labour strategy will be driven by the need for productivity improvements and that the emphasis will switch from continually recruiting in high labour turnover industries to retaining and developing employees. This will greatly enhance the prospects of improving both productivity and service as by implication, lower turnover is linked to job satisfaction. Further, the trend is for organizations to become more open and participative in management style. This represents a significant challenge for senior management as decision making in hospitality/tourism tends to be autocratic. Additionally, the image is one of low pay, long and unsocial hours and little functional flexibility. There is evidently a need to improve the level of technological uptake, the provision for flexible working and for multiskilled workers. In this, human resource managers will need to address the challenges associated with job design, work variety, self-autonomy and job enrichment.

Productivity in Japan (B: 43 pp 178-199)
Japan's economic success has inevitably led to the export of Japanese business philosophy and working practices, particularly in relation to performance improvement and total quality. In general, attitudes to business tend towards aggression and self-centredness in the West in contrast to Japanese nationalism and fierce loyalty to the company. Differences in economic performance relate to:
- *the role of government.* Successive Japanese governments have supported high technology industries by encouraging investment and international trade.
- *a long-term approach to strategy.* Western strategy is often designed to satisfy shareholders while the Japanese look for long-term corporate growth through the re-investment of profits.
- *the corporate philosophy.* Japanese corporate objectives are viewed as attainable challenges by a committed workforce who, in return for loyalty to the organization, play a full role in the life and development of the company. This in turn, explains comparatively high employee retention rates.
- *Wealth creation.* Western assets are usually derived from the astute buying and selling of businesses or shares, while the Japanese tend to view wealth as an internal commodity which must be nurtured naturally.
- *Employees.* Japanese companies encourage teamwork, job rotation and employee

participation through techniques like quality circles.

Resource strategies for the 1990s (A: 4 pp 65-69)
During the 1980s, two key resource strategies emerged:
- *Product-orientated strategies* in which all resources are considered as impersonal factors which contribute to the value chain.
- *Market-orientated* in which team-building is seen as the key to performance improvement.

The two approaches represent opposite ends of the spectrum and it likely that a range of intermediate positions will be taken-up by hospitality/tourism organizations seeking to improve performance and productivity using product-orientated techniques in combination with the team-building philosophy required to attain total quality management.

CONCLUSION

The hospitality industry has, in the past, tended to adopt a passive and traditional approach to business management which was appropriate in conditions of high demand and economic growth. More recently, demand and growth have slowed, thereby increasing pressures on senior management to utilize corporate resources more efficiently and effectively. At such times, it is tempting to approach the problem from a cost-reducing, contractive viewpoint, but lessons from Japan suggest that expansive, revenue-maximizing strategies may enhance prospects of long-term organizational growth and performance improvement.

References:

1. M.Porter, *Competitive Advantage: Creating and Sustaining a Superior Performance.* Free Press, New York, 1985.
2. G.Johnson & K.Scholes. *Exploring Corporate Strategy.* Prentice Hall, Hemel Hempstead, 1989.

Review questions:

1. Describe each of the primary and support activities of Porter's value chain and comment upon their implications for the hospitality and tourism industries.

2. Review some of the univariate financial methods used in hospitality/tourism and comment upon their advantages and limitations.

3. Write notes on the factors which are affecting human resource management in hospitality/tourism and the generic strategies which might be used in response.

EXTENSION

Read: Chapter 9 of *Managing Projects in Hospitality Organizations* (D: 9 pp 241-262)

Although the hospitality industry employs a significant number of people and provides excellent career opportunities, it could be argued that education and training has traditionally been viewed as a cost and not an investment. This chapter focuses upon the government's response via the National Council for Vocational Qualifications (NCVQ).

Extension questions:

1. Discuss the arguments you could use to convince senior managers that training is an investment and not a cost.

2. Outline ways in which the hospitality or tourism industry could work more closely with education and training organizations to achieve NCVQ objectives.

3. Discuss the future training needs of hospitality or tourism over the next ten years. What strategies should be developed to achieve these objectives?

Practical exercises:

1. Debate the merits and demerits of efficiency and effectiveness of resource utilization in the light of the current and foreseeable hospitality/tourism environments.

2. Select two companies from one sector of the hospitality or tourism industries and compare and contrast their different approaches to education and training. Support your review with published information and/or company budgets and training plans.

3. Investigate the resource management strategies used by an organization with which you are familiar and prepare a presentation outlining the changes which you would wish to recommend to the board of directors.

10 GENERATING AND EVALUATING OPTIONS

INTRODUCTION

"Rational analysis will enable the accepted scarce availability of creativity and judgement to be better exploited." P.G.Moore and H.Thomas, The Anatomy of Decisions. Penguin. London 1988.

Although strategic planning is sometimes depicted as a rational, systematic activity, it nonetheless requires strategists who can think analytically and creatively about the range of feasible options. Creativity is a cognitively demanding activity which engages both sides of the human brain. The right side is responsible for thought processes which are associated with creativity and innovation; the left side for regulating and organizing information in an ordered, logical way. A balance between the two functions is therefore essential to the selection of the best, most feasible business options.

In this chapter:
- *Generating options:*
- Creative thinking (B: 37 pp 154-157)
- Brainstorming (B: 38 pp 159-161)
- Problem solving (B: 39 pp 162-165)
- Mind mapping (B: 40 pp 166-169)
- Generating strategic development ideas (C: 9 pp 196-212)
- Competitive options (C: 9 pp 208-211)
- *Evaluating options* (C: 9 pp 212-225):
- Financial risk appraisal models (C: 9 pp 212-222)
- Strategic fit (C: 9 pp 222-223)
- Strategic fit ranking (C: 9 pp 223-224)

REVIEW

Creative thinking (B: 37 pp 154-157)
Scientists agree there are two main types of thinking; analytical (or convergent) and creative (or divergent):
- *Analytical thinking* assumes that there is a correct approach or answer to a problem and seeks to reach an appropriate solution in a logical, rational way.
- *Creative thinking* is more concerned with the generation of ideas and because of this, thinking is non-judgemental. Creative thinking tends to generate unconnected ideas and interaction with the individual's imagination may lead to the discovery of new connections between existing ideas.

Creativity is innate, but as the process of education emphasizes the importance of logic and the value of testing and examination, it is conceivable that the learner will not utilize knowledge in the most effective way. Further, the process of socialization generates psychological barriers to creative thinking as we learn to identify familiar patterns and to filter information in a logical and meaningful way. There are a number of ways in which individuals and organizations refine the collection and collation of information so that it can be reduced and interpreted according to established criteria:
- *Recipes* represent prior learning experiences which help us to think about and judge new situations or deal with an overload of information.
- *Repertoires* are collections of recipes which help individuals and organizations to process information, but in doing so, they may reduce the scope for creative thinking.
- *Evaluation and judgement* facilitate rapid categorization, even condemnation of new or fresh ideas without regard to the original insights that they might reveal. Familiarity is often more comfortable than invention and a preference for the known rather than the unknown may lead to the premature rejection of good ideas.
- *Satisficing* occurs when we accept a satisfactory solution to a problem rather than opting to continue the search for the optimal solution.
- *Mindset and assumptions* may represent a tendency to believe that our view of a given situation is the one and only realistic viewpoint, in which case, we are less likely to make an effort to see a different point of view. Conversely, an open mindset is more likely to stimulate creativity.

Brainstorming (B: 38 pp 159-161)
Brainstorming is a technique designed to stimulate creative thinking in the context of a disciplined group setting. Its purpose is to freely generate ideas, not to judge them, within a group comprised of participants with different backgrounds, viewpoints and expertise. A group facilitator should try to encourage participants to speak openly, so that a free-flowing discussion develops and in turn, stimulates creative thinking about different facets of the topic(s) under discussion. Ideas are generally

written down on flip-chart paper and then posted around the meeting room. At best, the views of all participants will be represented by encouraging informal, non-judgemental discussion.

Problem solving (B: 39 pp 162-165)
Whereas brainstorming focuses upon creative thinking so as to generate the maximum number of ideas, problem solving seeks to combine both creative and analytical thinking. The aim is to generate ideas, evaluate them and then arrive at a decision which is feasible to implement. This is a relatively complex process to control and confusion can arise if participants are unclear about the purpose of the meeting or find themselves simultaneously working on different facets or stages of the problem. Accordingly, clarification should be given by the facilitator at regular intervals so that participants are fully aware of resolutions made and the general progress of the meeting.

There are at least three key problem solving roles: *the client*, the person who has taken ownership of the problem and is seeking a solution; *the meeting leader or facilitator*, who is responsible for managing the meeting process, clarifying meaning and communicating resolutions and progress; *the participants*, who generate and evaluate ideas and proposals for implementation.

There are a number of guiding principles for running a problem solving group. *Choosing the group*: ensure that participants with the authority to approve or veto a decision are present at the meeting. *Preparation*: where possible, meet individually with the participants before the meeting in order to brief them. *Opening the meeting*: review the agenda and agree on the way in which the meeting will be conducted. *Stating the problem*: the client should provide an overview of the issues to be resolved, together with any factors or constraints which may impinge upon the organization, details of previously tried solutions and/or progress so far. *Idea generation*: a similar process to brainstorming, conducted within the time constraints of the agenda. *Choice of solution*: at the appropriate point, the facilitator should invite the client to select one or more of the ideas for more detailed discussion and analysis. *Strengths and weaknesses*: participants review each of the selected ideas in order to examine relative strengths and weaknesses. *Final choice*: towards the end of the meeting, the client and participants identify the most suitable option and if appropriate, consider implementation details.

Mind mapping (B: 40 pp 166-169)
The technique of mind mapping (1) facilitates the exploration of a wide range of ideas and lines of thought in a more comprehensive and systematic way than simply listing ideas in checklist style. Further, it can be used to assist in overcoming the tension which sometimes arises between the richness of thinking and related verbal and written communication which in business, can be confined by rules and conventions. The first step involves entering a word, drawing or symbol representing a particular theme at the centre of a page. As further thoughts occur, they are entered in the form of branches from the theme and as further elaboration takes place, a tree structure takes shape. Key ideas can be denoted by circles (or other coding conventions). The complete map depicts interrelationships and options which can be analyzed, re-structured or revised in the context of a small group meeting.

Generating strategic development ideas
(C: 9 pp.196-212)
As noted in chapter 7, conceptual frameworks or models can be of value to strategists in assessing business performance. There are a number of models which are more specifically orientated towards the evaluation of strategic direction. Several of these are noted below.

- *the product/market growth vector matrix,* devised by Ansoff (2) is illustrated in Figure 9.1 (C: 9 p 198). It proposes a review of profit-generating strategies in relation to the relative maturity of the organization's products and markets. Key considerations are: whether to divest, seek greater efficiency, market consolidation or penetration in mature markets characterized by mature products; whether to pursue market development in new markets with new products; whether to invest in product development in mature markets with new products; whether to diversify in new markets with new products.
- *focus strategies,* adovated by Peters and Waterman (3) are sometimes referred to as 'sticking to the knitting' and 'getting closer to customers'. In essence, they argue that market leaders are often service leaders too and a common characteristic is an obsession with quality. This translates into a desire to listen to customers, to exceed their expectations and a determination to remain focused upon existing business strengths.
- *the customer profitability matrix,* devised by Shapiro *et al* (4) is based on the premise that organizations tend to underestimate the earnings potential of specific market (or customer) segments. The matrix has four quadrants which could be used to review the revenue earning potential of products serving particular customer segments:

- *bargain basement,* for customers who seek limited added value service, but expect low-cost products with a relatively small profit margin;
- *passive,* for customers who are willing to pay premium prices without extensive service support;
- *carriage,* for trade customers who demand costly service inputs, but expect to pay a premium price for the service provided;
- *aggressive,* for customers representing large, highly professional organizations that place large orders yielding substantial profits but in return, expect total quality, extra service responsiveness and low prices.

There are a number of other profit-generating strategies which organizations could consider, these include: investing in growth markets; improving product quality in support of increased pricing and seeking synergistic benefits by combining two activities which yield a greater return than can be achieved by operating them independently. However, it should be noted that new strategic directions incur costs, notably the need to learn from experience, often referred to as the 'experience curve'. Evidence shows that the cost of undertaking a repetitive task decreases each time the volume of production doubles. Ultimately as organizations grow, cost savings arise from learning by experience, through specialization, product and process improvement, and by achieving economies of scale.

Competitive options (C: 9 pp 208-211)
It is possible to depict competitive options in relation to a continuum ranging from offensive, through collaborative and non-threatening to defensive moves. Offensive moves seek to achieve competitive advantage by creating new alignments of the organization with the industry's competitive forces. Collaborative or non-threatening tactics are aimed at improvements in the firm's market. Defensive moves are appropriate when a firm is threatened by a potential new entrant or by an existing rival seeking to encroach into its traditional market.

Evaluating options (C: 9 pp 212-225)
The choices eventually made with regard to strategic direction will involve the deployment of resources. Accordingly each option must be measured against its profit-generating potential.

Financial risk appraisal models (C: 9 pp 212-222)
The purpose of risk appraisal is to assist analysts in their efforts to quantify forecasts of the potential earnings, the resources required and the costs and risks associated with particular strategic options. Techniques include:

- *gap analysis*: where are we now and where do we want to be?
- *return on investment (ROI)*: used to evaluate the wealth-generating potential of a particular strategic option, which should provide a better rate of return than the risk-free market rate of interest.
- *discounted cash flow (DCF)*: an investment appraisal technique used to undertake a detailed analysis of the cash flow projections over the lifetime of the investment under review.
- *break-even analysis*: a cost-volume-profit technique which shows the impact of different levels of activity on the profitability of a potential investment.
- *payback period analysis*: concerned with liquidity and the speed with which investment expenditure is likely to be recouped. An investment that 'pays back' more quickly will tend to find favour over other, longer-term investments offering similar expected returns.
- *cash flow forecasts*: used to assess the liquidity position over a period of time.
- *sensitivity analysis*: involves the identification of key factors associated with the expected financial performance of a venture and, using spreadsheet analysis, reviewing 'what if' permutations. Typically, factors would include market demand, prices, costs and production levels.
- *simulation modelling*: extends the sensitivity analysis technique by assigning probability distributions to all key factors and then simulating the way factors might interact. The resultant model describes a range of outcomes, with probability values for each outcome.
- *scenario analysis*: represents an attempt to predict the possible future situations (or scenarios) that a firm might face so that the risks associated with the strategic options under review can be explored.
- *stakeholder support*: the success of a particular strategy often depends more upon the support it receives from stakeholders that on its inherent economic, profit-maximizing rationality. If key stakeholders find a particular strategic option unacceptable, it will almost certainly be difficult to implement.

Strategic fit (C: 9 pp 222-223)
Although financial feasibility is a crucial test, the organization must also consider the extent to which a particular strategic option fits with existing resources, structures and operations. The concept of corporate fit also reflects the extent to which a strategic option reflects an organization's culture and values and takes advantage of perceived strengths and opportunities.

Strategic fit ranking (C: 9 pp 223-224)
Having rationally estimated the profit-potential and organizational suitability of each strategic option, the final step is to weight them by using a ranking matrix. The value of such matrices will, inevitably, be limited by the individual interpretation of the weighting, but the very process of trying to quantify choice is in itself, an aid to rational and systematic decision-making.

CONCLUSION

Creative thinking is a fundamental requirement of the strategist, who must generate ideas, shape them into strategic options and evaluate them as objectively as possible. It is important to develop mechanisms for evaluating the feasibility, suitability and vulnerability of strategic options so that risks can be minimized or at least anticipated prior to implementation. The internal view of the best option is perhaps easier to establish than the likely reactions of external stakeholders such as customers and suppliers; this presents a challenge to organization's to consult widely and choose carefully.

References:

1. T.Buzan, *Use Your Head.* BBC Books, London, 1974.
2. H.Ansoff. *Corporate Strategy.* Penguin, Harmondsworth, 1968
3. T.Peters & R.Waterman. *In Search of Excellence.* Harper & Row, New York, 1982.
4. B.Shapiro, Y.Rangan, R.Moriarty & E.Ross.'Manage Your Customers for Profits (Not Just Sales), *Harvard Business Review,* Sept/Oct 1987; pp 101-8.

Review questions:

1. Review the barriers to creative thinking in organizations and suggest how they might be overcome.

2. Evaluate the utility of the models used to assist with the generation and evaluation of strategic options.

3. Evaluate the utility of the techniques used for financial risk appraisal and comment on the extent to which best options (from a financial standpoint) may conflict with wider organizational interests.

EXTENSION

Read: Chapter 12 of *Managing Projects in Hospitality Organizations* (D 12 pp 311-325)

The chapter is concerned with measures taken to develop creativity and innovative thinking in a division of Forte plc. The starting point was a recognition that while innovation is necessary, it is comparatively uncommon in large, international organizations. The chapter considers ways in which creativity could be approached through a case study of the implications of change at the Heathrow Posthouse.

Extension questions:

1. What are the benefits and disadvantages to managers, and the organization as a whole, of developing creativity?

2. To what extent do you thing that Forte's approach worked and is the progress sustainable? Is it necessary for well-established hospitality companies to be innovative?

3. How might an organization measure the level of innovation internally and the success of a programme aimed at increasing creativity levels among managers?

Practical exercises:

1. Debate the proposition: 'Creative managers, just like creative people in any walk of life, are born not made'.

2. Your task is to define a new product for a fast food restaurant chain of your choice using the brainstorming technique. Your group should continue in session until at least twenty ideas have been listed and explored. With the aid of a group observer, conclude the session with a review of the brainstorming process and nature of the interactions which occurred.

3. Identify the role that innovation plays in the management of a hospitality firm of your choice. Review its impact on the organizational structure, management roles and style, product development policy and the extent of its influence on the firm's competitive advantage.

11 STRATEGIES FOR CHANGE

INTRODUCTION

A constant feature of the business world is change; the comparative stability of the 1950s and 1960s gave way to increased global competition, rapid technological innovation, rising resource costs and many other types of change. This complicates the task of managing corporate change and the strategist is faced with the need to implement strategies which fit the organization's circumstances and ambitions as well as events influencing the economy, industry and sector in which the firm operates.

In this chapter:
- Turnaround (B: 27 pp 113-117)
- Consolidation
- Growth
- Expansion and multi-site operation (E: 9 pp 134-159; H: 9 pp 171-187 & H: 10 pp 188-207)
- Managing human resources and international expansion (E: 9 pp 144-147; H: 11 pp 208-239)
- Operational structures (E: 9 pp 151-154)

REVIEW

Turnaround (B: 27 pp 113-117)
Recovery or (turnaround) strategies are necessary when a business is in decline, often as a consequence of uncontrollable external events. Symptoms and causes of decline include: weak management; inadequate financial control; competitive weakness; a high cost structure; changes in market demand; ineffective marketing; commodity price fluctuations; project failure and overtrading. Inflexible, bureaucratic organizations are particular vulnerable, and appropriate courses of action may include the need to: adjust resources to changes in demand; monitor the external environment more closely and seek to become more adaptable; review gearing levels and borrowing commitments; widen the scope of decision making; recognize the inherent dangers in overtrading; learn from competitors.

Central to successful turnaround is acceptance by senior management of the problems arising from errors of judgement and/or strategic miscalculations.

If management accept responsibility, then it is more likely that plans can be reviewed and revised in a positive, constructive way. If not, ad hoc attempts to cut costs and/or rationalize may be viewed as rather desperate, defeatist measures which are likely to cause a further decline in corporate morale.

Slatter (1) notes that most successful turnaround situations are characterized by a change of the senior management responsible for the firm's failure and, equally seriously, for failing to respond to impending crisis. An incoming chief executive or managing director needs to demonstrate decisive leadership by setting realistic turnaround objectives and targets and appointing a team with clear roles and responsibilities to manage the turnaround at various levels in the organization.

There are a number of priorities for the initial turnaround period:
Short term (weeks 1-3): incoming management should assume financial control and seek fully to understand the sales situation. Departments should be required to submit cost-reduction recommendations and to justify existing costs.

Medium-term (weeks 3-8): implementation of a cost-reduction programme and the commencement of a detailed review of each department's contribution to the business, particularly focused upon ways in which systems and attitudes prevent effectiveness.

Longer-term (beyond week 8): the organization should seek to develop and implement an integrated recovery strategy, to include a revised budget, new project proposals, and team-building initiatives to raise morale and increase employee commitment to and participation in the recovery procress.

Slatter's study of corporate recovery identified a number of characteristics commonly associated with the successful implementation of turnaround strategies, including: successful asset reduction; a change of senior management; improved cash generation improved financial control; successful cost reduction; improved marketing; the implementation of organization changes.

Consolidation
The purpose of consolidation is to maintain market share in a dynamic environment and, therefore, it is not the same as doing nothing. For example, an organization operating in a growing market may prefer to consolidate its position rather incur extra costs and/or risks by challenging for the market leadership position. In a mature marketplace, consolidation may take the form of quality improvement or cost reduction in order to protect

market share. In declining markets, consolidation may require re-configuration of the value chain with a view to improving productivity. For example, this could be achieved by negotiating new sources of supply. Difficulties arise in determining if the market is in long or short term decline, and if turnaround cannot be quickly achieved, then a market exit strategy may be the only viable option.

Growth
For an organization to grow, it must gain market share by undertaking one or more of the following courses of action: improve its market penetration; develop and successfully launching new products; diversify; entering new markets; exploit new uses for its product(s); expand its operations into new geographical areas.

There are several models which seek to depict the impact of growth on the organization. Chandler (2) identifies four stages of organizational development arising from business growth: *expansion (first phase)*: to meet growing demand; *efficiency*: rationalizing the use of expanding resources; *expansion (second phase)*: continued growth through expansion with new products and new markets; *rationalization*: structural reorganization to ensure a better 'fit' between the new tasks facing the firm and its organizational structure.

Greiner's model (3) recognizes five phases of growth, each with organizational crisis points associated with growth in organizational size, complexity and maturity:
Phase 1: Growth through creativity. Product development and the selling activities of a small team bring about a crisis of leadership for the owner/operator as growth reaches the point beyond which employees can be managed by informal processes.
Phase 2: Growth through direction. The need to systemize and formalize procedures due to increasing size and/or complexity may lead to the over-centralization of decision making. This can cause a crisis of autonomy as employees react against the increasing formality.
Phase 3: Growth through delegation. Measures to increase employee participation may lead to a crisis of executive control as managers and supervisors assume greater responsibility for decisions relating to their organizational role.
Phase 4: Growth through coordination. Formal systems designed with corporate integration in mind, tend to give rise to excessive 'red tape'.
Phase 5: Growth through collaboration. Team-working, matrix structures and real-time information systems are used to overcome bureaucracy, and self-managed teams replace more formalized control mechanisms.

Expansion and multi-site operation (E: 9 pp 134-159; H: 9 pp 171-187 & H: 10 pp 188-207)
Hospitality/tourism businesses normally provide services which are concentrated at the point of consumption. Consequently, this means that expansion decisions involve increasing the number of multi-site operations and the geographical distribution of units. Factors influencing expansion decisions include:
- locational choice and site acquisition;
- localized and/or regional markets as defined by the catchment area;
- operational complexity - standardized operations are generally easier to replicate;
- supply lines, logistics and potential savings arising from economies of scale;
- product differentiation - the potential to increase distribution of a recognized brand.

Although geographically dispersed units may benefit from the replication of standardized design concepts, product configurations and systems, variations in localized supply and demand must be taken into account. Further, the organization as a whole must adjust by adapting or augmenting communication and control networks and other forms of technical and specialist support.

A decision to expand internationally may arise from a desire to sustain organic development, particularly as home markets mature, and the need to establish a presence in growth markets becomes self-evident. At this point, a number of key factors should be fully considered. They include:
- the compatibility of the company's products/services with the prospective overseas market(s);
- the size and accessibility of overseas target markets and the marketing, sales and distribution channel networks required to achieve satisfactory levels of market penetration;
- social, economic and cultural differences and the associated implications for operating an overseas business;
- the prospects for establishing satisfactory distribution relationships with indigenous sales agencies and/or partnerships with overseas companies via a strategic alliance or joint venture;
- arrangements for procurement and supply so as to ensure consistent operating standards, guaranteed prices and supply and potential benefits which may accrue from establishing an overseas supply network;

- product development and research implications;
- finance and control implications;
- human resource implications, with particular reference to localized labour markets, recruitment, training and development.

Structurally, a multinational hospitality organization may resemble its national counterpart but management policies, practices and procedures need to reflect regional and local conditions. In this regard, managers can learn from each other and experience personal growth within the context of international operations; an opportunity which is greatly valued by the Hyatt International Corporation:

"Hyatt managers are constantly exposed to a variety of cultural perspectives in discussions spanning a wide range of issues. Consequently, new policies and procedures are tested against multinational views to identify the possible implications arising from implementation in different places." (E: 19 p 344)

International development requires a responsive and flexible corporate attitude towards the extent of control which is exercised from the centre of the organization so that sufficient scope exists for decision making at the local level. This may represent a fundamental change to the way in which the organization normally operates. However, country-specific legislation on land ownership, building regulations, company formation, employment law and many other legal, fiscal, linguistic, political and social differences necessitates a degree of self-autonomy for overseas operating divisions. In this way, effective policies can be determined for managing change associated with currency exchange and interest rates, pricing, fluctuations in the cost of finance and the impact of different social structures and cultures on service quality and performance.

Managing human resources and international expansion (E: 9 pp 144-147; H: 11 pp 208-239)
The skills and abilities of an organization's human resources play a key role in facilitating international growth. Watson and Litteljohn (E: 9 p 145 Table 9.3) cite three generic strategies which, depending on the size of the company and its structure, the degree of internationalization and its long-term strategies, can be used to manage change during expansion:

Ethnocentric: The organization employs the same strategies and practices in every country in which it operates and places emphasis on centralized systems of decision-making. Managers are recruited and developed in the home country for deployment anywhere in the world.

Polycentric: Human resource management is decentralized on a country by country basis so as to take into account local environments. Managers are trained and developed within the locality in which they work.

Geocentric: Human resources are managed on a global basis so as to harmonize development needs wherever they arise and to remain responsive to local operating environments. This strategy encourages the development of the best people from anywhere in the world for key positions within the company as a whole.

In order to evolve an international ethos, the organization must ensure that it can meet current and foreseeable human resource needs. A current trend in international companies is to remove a layer of middle management at the unit level. This can lead to greater competition for fewer jobs, but it also has the effect of encouraging individual managers to take greater responsibility for their self-development. International organizations should, however, retain responsibility for employee training in cultural awareness (including language training) so as to promote and sustain an international outlook and interest. As noted earlier, Hyatt seek to expose their managers to an array of issues relating to their work by actively encourage individual units to participate in gathering data on international events:

"When for example, the complex process of change began to gain momentum in Eastern Europe, details of development opportunities began to emerge instinctively from all parts of the global organization. The information came from managers at all levels in the organization who were either witnessing change or gathering market information from talking to business travellers and others with experiential knowledge of what was actually happening." (E: 19 p 342.)

Operational structure (E: 9 pp.151-154)
In considering options for operating and controlling an expanding business, it is necessary to assess the appropriateness of the three main methods of operation: direct ownership of resources, management contracting and franchising.
- *Direct ownership*: the organization retains complete ownership and control of the business but in doing so, must take full responsibility for securing the resources to fund operations. The high level of investment and expertise required for this type of structure may be alleviated by taking on a partner. A partnership or alliance may, however, run into difficulties if the respective corporate cultures conflict or problems arise regarding the question of strategic control.

- *Management contracting*: allows growth at a much faster rate than asset ownership. The operating company provide the necessary expertise to run a commercially viable business and the property owners generally take responsible for maintaining the property to an agreed standard.
- *Franchising*: normally requires the provision of a full support network for an established brand. Typically this includes training in business methods, assistance with the development of key staff, marketing and advertising expertise and help in setting up the business. Development and associated costs are met by the investor.

CONCLUSION

The many types of change which affect businesses often determine the strategic responses which organizations make. In crisis situations, a turnaround strategy, can, if it is radical enough, facilitate corporate recovery. In recession, consolidation and/or rationalization may be needed to reduce costs and stem sources of loss. In some respects, the most complex of all responses to environmental conditions is to expand. This often has far-reaching consequences for the change processes within the organization, especially if international expansion is to succeed. Above all, organizations depend upon the efforts of their employees, and the key to successful expansion in home and overseas markets is to recognize and respond to changing human resource needs.

References:

1. S.Slatter. *Corporate Recovery: A Guide to Turnaround Management.* Penguin, London, 1984.
2. A.Chandler. *Strategy and Structure.* MIT Press, Boston, MA. 1962.
3. L.Greiner. 'Evolution and revolution as Organizations Grow.' *Harvard Business Review.* July-August, 1972.

Review questions:

1. Outline the reasons for corporate decline and suggest ways in which a turnaround strategy could be implemented in an organization of your choice.
2. Identify and explain the economic factors which might cause hospitality/tourism organizations to opt for consolidation, rationalization and expansion respectively.
3. Examine the relevance of generic human resource strategies with examples drawn from hospitality and tourism.

EXTENSION

Read: Chapter 6 of *Managing Projects in Hospitality Organizations* (D: 6 pp 146-168)

In planning strategies for change, managers often face additional pressures from the need to meet productivity targets and control production costs. The chapter focuses on the process of technological change arising from the introduction of *sous vide* production at Scott's Hotels. In turn, this has wide-ranging implications for changes in materials measurement, working methods and employee attitudes.

Extension questions:

1. Evaluate the applicability of the productivity strategy options shown in Figure 6.2 and Table 6.1 (D: 6 p 150). to examples drawn from the literature and your own experience.
2. Examine the distinction between job training and the attitude change which some companies seek to instil in their employees. Which of these two styles best describes Scott's induction of chefs and which is likely to be the more healthy for the company?
3. Can the work of a kitchen be analyzed scientifically? Are there any realistic means of increasing the efficiency of labour, apart from using technology such as *sous vide*?

Practical exercises:

1. Investigate how productivity is measured in a hospitality/tourism unit with which you are familiar and comment on the recommendations you would make in the light of your investigation.
2. Investigate the proposition that *sous-vide* is better suited to bureaucratic-type organizations than to those with organic structures and self-directed work groups.
3. Prepare a role-play exercise in which you, the manager of a hotel like the Garden Court/Courtyard described in the case, interview an applicant with a very traditional background for the job of chef.

12 PLANNING FOR CHANGE

INTRODUCTION

"...the most significant issue facing hospitality firms during this decade will be how to accomplish the change in thinking necessary to develop operations-oriented unit-level managers into strategic-thinking managers." M.D.Olsen, (IJCHM, v3n4, 1991, p. 24.)

Change is a reality of organizational life for hospitality/tourism firms in the 1990s. The complexity of the external environment, combining recession, intense competition, turbulent markets and other change factors, also requires greater managerial flexibility, responsiveness and a willingness to adapt to different styles of working. This implies cultural change too, so that individuals and groups can re-focus their roles and, at the same time, seek ways of improving customer service.

In this chapter:
- Organizational change (A: 12 pp 195-204)
- Initiating change (B: 16 pp 64-67; B: 18 pp 70-73; C: 8 pp 179-183)
- Forte PLC: Appraising the organizational impact of change (E: 10 pp 167-170)
- Cultural change in organizations (C: 3 pp 57-60; E: 17 pp 296-311)
- Hilton International: Creating a service-driven culture

REVIEW

Organizational change (A: 12 pp 195-204)
To survive and prosper, all types of organizations must engage in two forms or strands of change activity:

- *Managing or adjusting internal affairs.* Managing internal operations requires a willingness and capacity to undertake a continuous stream of internal adjustments. These may be carried out by individuals and teams of people working at different levels, and the task is one of reconciling projected or budgeted targets with actual performance. Examples include action taken to monitor and adjust activity in line with operational plans and standards (quality, productivity, profitability) ensuring that quotas met and benchmarks achieved. Ideally, internal adjustments should reinforce the distinctiveness of the organization, its operating strengths, the optimal use of resources and the specific skills of its employees. Consistency of adjustment tends to preserve organizational coherence and supports the second strand of change; responding to changes in the external environment.

- *Responding to the external environment.* All organizations are environmentally dependent with respect to resources, markets, and satisfying their external constituencies. As environments change, organizations need to realign themselves (see chapter 14) and response capability is likely to depend upon a commitment to pro-active environmental scanning so that trends can be identified and change needs anticipated. Looking back, it is possible to track the impact of external changes on the strategies deployed by international hotel companies. In the 1970s catalysts for change included: (a) the growing influence of North American hospitality firms and, (b) internationalization. In the 1980s, the changes in the external environment were more rapid and numerous. They included: (a) diminishing US influence; (b) growth by acquisition; (c) more varied forms of internationalization; (d) a greater focus on financial management; (e) improved market segmentation and, (f) a greater emphasis on developed markets.

Initiating change (B: 16 pp 64-67; B: 18 pp 70-73; C: 8 pp 179-183)
Change processes in organizations are often difficult to implement and unpopular with employees because they are disruptive, sometimes unpredictable and because individuals or groups of people may feel threatened by change. It is therefore important to try to anticipate the barriers and objections posed by those with an interest in maintaining the status quo. Resistance to change in organizations generally occurs on three levels:
- *Rational.* Sources include: a belief that the change itself and/or the timing is wrong or the methods inappropriate; resistance due to lack of consultation; failure of prior change(s) resulting in a lack of confidence; a belief that management and/or the organization lack the ability to implement the change; lack of appeal due to little or no perceived personal gain from the proposed change.

- *Emotional.* Sources include: resistance due to the implied criticism of the way things are currently done (especially if those responsible for the task(s) under review were involved in defining the process); low levels of trust due to broken promises or a suspicion that the desire for change is motivated by a hidden agenda (such as staff reductions); lack of self-confidence in coping with change and/or fear of failure; a preference for stability (rather than turbulence); lack of understanding about the reasons and/or implications of the change.

- *Political.* Sources include: a fear of losing power, status, authority, freedom; a belief that the importance of specific skills will be eroded and that jobs may be lost; peer pressure to resist change.

In seeking to overcome resistance to change, it is helpful to devise a statement of the desired end state and to disseminate this to those who will be directly or indirectly affected. This helps to reduce levels of anxiety, establish a clear target for organizational change and provide opportunities for constructive debate and discussion. Additionally, it may help to engender a sense of progress and purpose on which people can build in an optimistic, forward-looking way.

There are a number of key tasks associated with initiating a change process:

- *Defining the current situation.* A case for change can be made more convincingly if it contains a realistic assessment of the current position. This should include a review of current strengths and weaknesses, organizational resources and capabilities and a comparison of the current situation with the desired end state. To this end, a resource audit checklist (see for example, C: 8 pp 180-181) can be used to identify the implications of change and, by disseminating all or part of the assessment via planning meetings, a common point of reference is established.

- *Planning change.* A change plan should include a communication schedule (who will be told what, when and how often), an activity schedule (what must be done, by whom, within what time-frame) and measurable objectives so that progress can be assessed as objectively as possible. Further, the plan should fully address how change will be achieved in relation to: (a) formal technical systems (equipment, systems, technology and operating procedures); (b) formal structures (subordinate-superior relationships, changes in responsibilities, status, rewards); (c) informal structures (the affects of change on factions and coalition groups within the organization).

- *Assessing probabilities.* Prior to implementing change, it is essential to assess the implications in terms of: (a) winners (those that gain from the change) how can they be used to facilitate change? (b) losers (of power, authority, status, respect) how will they resist the changes, what can be done to reduce this source of opposition? (c) uncertainties - how can misunderstandings be avoided?

- *Selecting the change facilitator(s).* The person(s) responsible for managing the change process should be given: (a) the authority to implement change if discussion and negotiation fail to overcome resistance; (b) sufficient resources to carry out the change. Additionally, the task requires the necessary interpersonal skill to negotiate and sell ideas and to generate enthusiasm and respect.

- *Implementation.* To accomplish change, it is often necessary to use a variety of management styles and tactics ranging from participative to coercive. Action may include: (a) education and communication (encourages a shared diagnosis of why and how); (b) participation and involvement (encourages ownership of the change process); (c) help and support (confidence-building, advice and support); (d) negotiation and agreement (compromise to overcome resistance); (e) manipulation (presentation of gains from complying with change, downplaying of losses); (f) coercion (threat of sanctions if non-compliant).

Forte PLC: Appraising the organizational impact of change (E: 10 pp 167-170)
Following the announcement of the 'building on strength strategy' in mid-1991, work on the new Forte brand structure took two years to complete. An exercise of this scale and importance could have faced resistance to change among many other sources of difficulty, and so it was deemed essential to sell the approach consistently and clearly throughout the organization and implement the change using fresh, innovative methods. Accordingly, implementation involved a number of carefully planned, sequential steps, including the preparation of:

- *an action programme* - identifying critical points in relation to deadline dates;
- *a refurbishment programme* - linked to re-defined design features and services for each hotel brand and collection type;

- *a 'key communicators' programme* - to implement an internal communication strategy involving a cascade of information about the practical implications of the strategy.

The group as a whole is benefiting from improvements to all its communication channels because of the success of its implementation plan. Further, there is a better sense of structure and cohesion arising from the perception that a dynamic step forward has been successfully completed.

Cultural change in organizations
(C: 3 pp 57-60; E: 17 pp 296-311)
"The stronger the cultural core of a firm, the more it is resistant to modification and the more the culture will persist in the face of a beleaguering environment". C. Lundberg & R.Woods (IJCHM, v2n4, 1990, p.6)

Achieving cultural change is generally considered to be a lengthy, expensive and difficult process, especially in relatively static cultures, where the change process will need to be initiated at chief executive level. Conversely, organizations with an embedded belief in the value of adapting to the external environment, will tend to view change as a natural, organic process. Nonetheless, cultural change has a significant impact on organizational life as its influence pervades thinking at all levels in the structural hierarchy and influences many aspects of business activity.

To some extent, cultural change should mirror the nature of change taking place in the external environment. Organizational implications could be assessed according to a typology consisting of: (a) steady state (i.e. no change); (b) gradual change, built on existing knowledge and skills; (c) gradual change, built on new knowledge and skills; (d) incremental change, built on existing knowledge and skills; (e) incremental change built on new knowledge and skills; (f) revolutionary change.

Deal and Kennedy (1) estimate that the cost of cultural change equates to between five and ten percent of the organization's annual budget and so profit improvement and/or cost reduction should form part of the overall objective. They suggest that the cultural change process should:
- recognize the importance of peer group consensus. If a team share a belief in the need for a given change, it is more likely to succeed;
- convey and emphasize two-way trust in communications so as to avoid the risk of misunderstandings;
- ensure that employees have been sufficiently well trained and prepared to implement the changes and make them work;
- allow sufficient time for completion of each phase of the change process.
- encourage employees to think of how they can adapt to meet the ideal change scenario.

Change implications for individuals and work groups can be assessed according to a number of criteria. These include: (a) organizational stability; (b) occupational value differentials; (c) training needs; (d) knowledge requirements; (e) intergroup relations; (f) morale; (g) rewards (E: 17 p.303).

Kilmann (2) offers a five step process to guide cultural change: (a) identify existing norms that guide behaviour and attitudes; (b) identify the ideal behaviours and the how they might be implanted; (c) create new behavioural norms (e.g. 'cost consciousness' so that tendencies towards dysfunctional behaviour are replaced; (d) use a survey to identify the cultural gap (the gap is normally narrower at the top and wider at the bottom of the organizational hierarchy); (e) close the culture gap by disseminating the information gathered and rewarding new behaviours and attitudes.

Hilton International: Creating a service-driven culture
Following the acquisition of Hilton International by Ladbroke in 1987, two research studies were commissioned to help identify the direction in which its service culture should develop. The results of the two studies, concerned with customer usage and attitudes and employee attitudes respectively, confirmed a need to:
- *Achieve greater customer-orientation.* A communication programme was implemented using videos, staff magazines, posters and new uniform insignia. A total of 54,000 employees worldwide, attended launch parties, flag raisings and presentations.

- *Reassert Hilton's brand presence and personality through advertising.* A new advertising campaign, translated into nine languages, was seen by an estimated 54 million people worldwide.

- *Improve training support to help employees to meet customer needs.* A series of 'service promises' were devised and over a nine month period, every employee in the company participated in the Hilton promise process. This involved writing and translating support materials, setting up local implementation teams and running three-day training meetings to encourage employees to measure the quality of work in their department and suggest ways of improving working conditions and practices. M.Hirst (IJCHM, v4n1, 1992, pp i-iii.)

The cultural shift in service-focus has, since its inception gained momentum, based on: (a) management commitment, support and involvement; (b) employee participation (c) equal attention to internal and external customer needs; (d) teamworking; (e) an emphasis on attention to detail; (f) recognizing achievements; (g) continual review and updating of service standards.

CONCLUSION

The complexity of factors directly or indirectly influencing the acceptance of change in organizations requires careful planning and review. Above all, an assessment of the sources of resistance and the tactics needed to minimize disaffection and disruption should permeate thinking and planning prior to, and during, each phase of the change process. In turn, this helps to promote organizational sensitivity to the implications of change and the best options for engendering a supportive cultural climate.

Review questions:

1. Identify and briefly describe an organizational change situation in which you were involved as either an observer, participant or initiator of change. Comment on the rational, emotional and political reactions of colleagues and on the action taken to respond to their concerns.

2. Select two hospitality/tourism organizations (one large, one small) and prepare a key task analysis checklist for initiating a change designed to reduce operating costs. Comment on the differences of approach needed and the organizational implications.

3. Review the benefits and problems associated with cultural change and identify the steps that you would take to close the cultural gap and implant new behavioural norms in an organization with which you are familiar.

References:

1. T.Deal and A.Kennedy. *Corporate Cultures*. Penguin, London, 1982.
2. R.L.Kilmann. *Beyond the Quick Fix*. Jossey-Bass, San Francisco, 1984.

EXTENSION

Read: Chapters 2 and 6 of *Achieving Quality Performance: Lessons from British Industry* (G)

Chapter 2 addresses the action taken by Cambell Lee Computer Services (CLCS) to achieve a cultural change focused on a total quality work ethos.

Chapter 6 provides an account of the planning for change needed to implement Prudential Assurance's (PA) 'Way of Life' (WoL) programme.

Extension questions (Chapter 2)

1. Assess the effectiveness of the action taken by CLCS to overcome conflicting pressures and secure employee commitment to their quality improvement programme (QIP).

2. Comment on the mechanisms developed by CLCS to enable individuals and teams to gain a better understanding of customer needs.

Practical exercises:

1. What action is needed to establish shared cultural values, attitudes and behaviours in an organizational setting? Drawing on the material in chapter 2, comment on the role they play in aiding or hindering the implementation of a QIP.

2. As chief executive, how would you establish a shared vision of customer service in an organization of your choice? How would this influence the process of change to achieve the desired level of service?

Extension questions (Chapter 6)

1. Assess the effectiveness of the preparation for organizational change at PA relating to its total quality management (TQM) programme.

2. Comment on the strengths and weaknesses of PA's approach to implementing TQM.

Practical exercises:

1. How might a hospitality/tourism firm benefit from a study of the change process at PA?

2. If asked, how would you modify the WoL programme to fit the operational characteristics of a hospitality/tourism firm of your choice? How should it be implemented?

13 MONITORING BUSINESS STRATEGY

INTRODUCTION

"Firms seem to measure only what is easy to measure, such as productivity and cost, and neglect measurement and control of other factors that are vital to the firm's competitive success." C.Voss, R.Johnston, L.Fitzgerald and R.Sylvestro (F: 7 p. 110).

The view of decision-making adopted in chapter 2 is that theoretical models can help to structure systematic, balanced and objective approaches to the process of strategic planning. In practice, the ease with which a plan or strategy can be implemented is a key consideration, and in this regard, the actions and procedures required to monitor progress are closely connected. Ultimately, a successful outcome will depend upon a combination of informed decision-making and planning, effective implementation and careful, sensitive monitoring using the most appropriate measures and indicators.

In this chapter:
- Theoretical approaches to the implementation of strategy (C: 10 pp 229-241 & H: 4 pp 70-91)
- Monitoring and feedback (C: 10 pp 235-236)
- A process-based model for monitoring business performance (F: 7 pp 110-118)
- The change process in practice (B: 19 pp 74-77)
- Control systems
- Regulatory systems

REVIEW

Theoretical approaches to the implementation of strategy (C: 10 pp 229-241 & H: 4 pp 70-91)
In many organizations, the core beliefs commonly held by managers shape the implementation of strategy and underlying beliefs and attitudes may need to be 'unfrozen' or modified before strategic change can occur.

Johnson (1) notes that there are broadly three styles of decision-making associated with the process of strategic management:

- *rationalistic,* analytical and rational decision-making, but often lacking in pragmatism;
- *incremental,* or step-by-step progress which closely mirrors the piecemeal way in which management decisions are often taken;
- *interpretative,* the application of 'recipes' to the solution of problems.

Rational decision-making implies the existence of a corporate mission, from which objectives can be set and quantified in the form of targets, and monitored during and after the implementation of strategy. In reality, the role and influence of the mission statement may be unclear, with senior management exerting influence in accordance with current priorities and pressures.

The pace of change as directed by external factors and the organization's needs and aspirations, may account for misperceptions of strategic direction. In this respect, senior management must take responsibility for periodic re-alignments to ensure that corporate objectives are fully understood throughout the organization and that incremental change is communicated clearly and consistently.

The rational model has a number of limitations, mainly arising from assumptions that highlight a gap between theory and practice:

- *decision need* is assumed although in fact, supporting evidence is rarely given full consideration except in crisis situations when circumstances (need) require an immediate and carefully considered response (decision).

- *problem definition* is often difficult to articulate with precision, simply because problems are rarely simple or straightforward. Perceptions of cause and effect vary enormously due to individual differences and organizational complexity. However, team-building methods and problem-solving techniques can be used to increase awareness of the problem definition issue.

- *relevant information* can be difficult, time-consuming and expensive to obtain and so managers routinely face the need to compromise on information needs and compensate by exercising personal judgement.

- *strategic alternatives* are rarely evenly balanced in terms of quality of information pertaining to assessment criteria. Inevitably this gives rise to subjective differences of opinion on best fit options, associated risks and implications.

- *the exercising of discretion* is difficult to avoid as most organizations allow or encourage scope for managers to exercise judgement so as to promote personal development and enable managers to respond to the organizational sub-strata of objectives.

Monitoring and feedback (C: 10 pp 235-236)
The procedures used to monitor and review courses of action taken at corporate or business unit level serve to provide the means of measuring the achievement of objectives. In this sense, they facilitate a cyclical process by enabling the refinement of objectives and subsequent planning activity. In practice however, operational complexities and timescales often mitigate against reflection and review and, unless a particular course of action has proved an overwhelming success or failure, accurate and precise feedback may be difficult to obtain. Additionally, complications can arise in defining an acceptable outcome, measuring performance and distinguishing long-term trends from short-term fluctuations.

While strategic decision models can assist with the analysis of individual stages, an overview of the entire process needs to be obtained. If the period between strategic choice, implementation and feedback is short, with little or no backtracking, an overview is comparatively easy to obtain. However, circumstances vary greatly and in large organizations, typically monitoring many different initiatives simultaneously, the strategic picture is much harder to interpret. In this respect, non-executive directors can play a valuable role in providing an objective analysis of the inter-play between spheres of corporate activity.

A process-based model for monitoring business performance (F: 7 pp 110-118)
Voss *et al.* cite three types of measures for service performance: cost, 'hard' performance (measures of performance that are easily quantified) and 'soft' performance (performance measures that are not easily quantified. They propose a process-based model (see Figure 7.1, F: 7 p. 113) for measuring five component parts of service performance. Key questions are as follows:
- *Process* - has the service process been designed according to specification and is it being operated as specified?

- *Productivity* - are specified standards for labour and plant/facilities productivity being met and properly measured?

- *Process inputs* - have appropriate measures relating to quality of human resources and materials been established and how are they maintained?

- *Process outputs* - how should service levels be specified and monitored in terms of hard and/or soft (intangible) measures? How should company and customer ratings of service levels be reconciled?

- *Financial control* - have appropriate measures been established to monitor costs, profits (or margins) and price performance at unit and corporate levels?

- *Market measures* - how should the service impact be monitored and measured in relation to the marketplace? (A wide variety of measures exist, from market share to sales levels.)

The change process in practice (B: 19 pp 74-77)
A change programme is generally most vulnerable around the half-way point in its implementation. By this time the investment has been made, co-ordinating groups set up and courses of action taken. The concerns arising tend to focus on whether the strategy is succeeding and if the evidence is limited, doubts may begin to surface. Managers should prepare their subordinates for this possibility, while aiming to achieve some small, early and easily identifiable successes.

The theory of force-field analysis proposes that in any change situation there are likely to be driving forces in favour of change and restraining forces opposed to change. Accordingly, the purpose of the analysis is to provide a clearer view of the driving and restraining forces and their relative strengths. A deliberate strengthening of the driving forces associated with the implementation of a given strategy can lead to a stiffening of the restraining forces. To avoid this, a determined effort to reduce the impact of restraining forces at the outset may improve the prospects for successful implementation. This should include the establishment of realistic, attainable objectives and the rationale for the intended course of action should be clear, easily comprehensible and often repeated.

Throughout the period of implementation, a continual stream of adjustments may need to be made to contend with unforeseen circumstances and to respond postively to suggestions from personnel involved in the process.

A potential source of conflict arises from a duplication of roles. If the same person or team of people formulate and implement policy, restraining influences in the form of dissent are likely to be viewed as attacks on the policy itself. A possible solution is to allocate different tasks and responsibilities to team members so that adjustments can be made without unduly weakening the case for change or the ensuing process of implementation.

An effective way of defusing restraining forces on a strategically important project is to launch what might best be described as a tactical, counter-culture offensive. This is essentially an exceptional course of action in which senior management override the way in which things normally happen. It is perhaps best exemplified by a direct appeal from senior management to the workforce. This may take the form of an open meeting for all employees in which senior management outline the reasons for a particular course of action and seek to gain a concensus of support.

Control systems
"...systems should concentrate on outputs and not on the detail of control over inputs. The industry has a tendency to over-control and lose sight of what is really important." P.R.Gamble (IJCHM, v3 n1, 1991, p. 16.)

The successful implementation of strategy requires a means of identifying progress so that appropriate corrective action can be taken to minimize the impact of sources of variance. Management information for this purpose typically includes:
- *market analysis*: To monitor changes in the market or differences in the market share achieved;
- *sales analysis*: To measure the extent to which sales budgets are being achieved;
- *physical resource analysis*: To assess the utilization of plant and materials;
- *human resource analysis*: To examine the productivity and stability of the workforce.

Systems design should ideally facilitate real-time (instant access) analysis of performance data so that the time lag between monitoring, adjustment and corrective action is as small as possible. Rocco Forte, Chairman and chief executive of Forte views this as a key organizational function:

"Computer-based real-time analysis of detailed management information has largely replaced manual methods, so that at the touch of a button it is possible to review the contribution made by different customer types in every unit of a division. This level of sophistication is able to support a variety of strategic decisions..." (A: 1 p.7).

Further, it is sensible to try to link monitoring activity to key or critical success factors and ratios so that variances can be quickly identified, prioritized and dealt with accordingly. Rocco Forte confirms this:

"It is not possible to run a business effectively today without the aid of key performance indicators and ratios. The management statistics used by Forte have been continually refined as information technology has developed, so that relatively sophisticated measures of business performance are now available. Additionally, there is greater emphasis today on short-term forecasting at an operational level, so that costs can be adjusted in relation to expected demand two or three weeks beforehand. This is an important initiative because simultaneous adjustments or even retrogressive cost-cutting to offset the effects of an unexpected shortfall in demand are relatively unhelpful options. " (A: 1 p. 7.)

The speed and accuracy of monitoring and review can be enhanced by the compartmentalization of performance data. It is useful, for example, to identify and create financial cost centres for small divisions or units within an organization so that responsibility can be attributed accordingly.

Regulatory systems
The effects of uncertainty and ambiguity, commonly associated with organizational change, can be mitigated by training and development designed to support personal growth in capabilities and confidence. Beyond this, a desire for organizational cohesion will be better supported if change agents are operating throughout the organization, perhaps in the form of a change task force (2).

To overcome the problem of 'organizational mind-set', many companies employ consultants to implant fresh ideas. In turn, this may stimulate the re-structuring of teams and working practices, effectively re-vitalizing the organization. In order to sustain organizational renewal and in particular, a fresh commitment to making things happen, recognition and reward systems have an important role to play. Ultimately they may help to re-align attitudes, behaviours and the driving force which is so crucial to organizational success.

CONCLUSION

Monitoring and evaluation, the final tasks associated with the implementation of strategy are crucially important because they provide a focal point for reinforcing success or, if poorly executed, opposition and criticism. The application of techniques such as force-field analysis to gauge resistence and real-time systems to highlight operational variances as and when they occur, requires a willingness to act decisively and a determination to promote organizational flexibility and sensitivity. This might be likened to a balancing act with sufficient momentum to maintain forward direction, stability and overcome the natural desire for inertia and the maintenance of the status quo.

References:

1. G.Johnson. *Strategic Change and the Management Process.* Basil Blackwell, Oxford, 1987.
2. H.Minzberg. *The Structuring of Organizations.* Prentice-Hall, Englewood Cliffs, NJ. 1979.

Review questions:

1. To what extent do organizations that you have worked for exhibit rationalistic, incremental or interpretative styles of decision-making? What in your opinion constitutes the best combination? Justify your view with reference to the size, structure and complexity of your example organization(s).

2. Using the process-based model developed by Voss *et al*, evaluate and appraise the service performance of an organization of your choice. Aim to identify any gaps in service performance and in response, prepare a set of recommendations to guide action on improvement and feeback.

3. Reflect on the strategic implications of the theory of force-field analysis by identifying respective driving and restraining forces in a hospitality or tourism organization with which you are familiar.

4. Evaluate the importance of real-time control systems in monitoring the implementation of business strategy and design a business information system for an organization of your choice. Include a rationale for the component parts and costs involved.

EXTENSION

Read: Chapter 11 of *Managing Projects in Hospitality Organizations* (D: 11 pp 290-310).

The chapter describes the dilemma facing the YMCA with regard to the commerical viability of its Castlefield hotel operation. The Castlefield is a small hotel, operated on traditional lines, and the case underlines the problems which organizations may face when they step out of their particular 'core' field of expertise. The chapter illustrates the way in which organizational inertia can inhibit the decision-making process and in this instance, the conceptualization and implementation of a viable commercial plan.

Extension questions:

1. Propose a strategy to assure the long term viability of the Castlefield hotel and indicate what information would be needed to monitor its effective implementation.

2. To what extent are commercial objectives and methods of operation compatible with non-commercial and charitable objectives? Relate your answer to the ethical standards and social responsibilities of business.

3. Consider and comment on the techniques that could have been utilized by the YMCA to improve its decision-making.

Practical exercises:

1. Prepare a three year business plan for a hospitality or tourism business with which you are familiar or for the educational establishment in which you are studying.

2. Select a hospitality or tourism organization and using published information, evaluate its performance over a five year period. Comment on its responsiveness to change and outline your recommendations for future strategy appropriate to its size, positioning, mission statement and objectives.

3. Examine and evaluate the competitive structure of the local hotel or restaurant and prepare a report on future prospects and potential.

14 ACHIEVING STRUCTURE AND STRATEGY CO-ALIGNMENT

INTRODUCTION

"The pace of change is quickening and firms that have adapted their thinking to new environments are staying healthy and prospering. Those that are not are sinking fast. It will become an industry characterized by a survival of the fittest not the fastest growing. The fittest will be those who are most successful in matching their strategy and structure in the context of the challenging environment." M.D.Olsen (IJCHM, v1n2, 1989, p.6)

Alignment is concerned with the fit between the organization's structure, processes, procedures, strategies and the markets it seeks to serve. Of fundamental importance is the way in which the organization interprets and reacts to environmental change. In order to maintain alignment in the 1990s, hospitality/tourism firms will need to monitor current events and trends, identify potential long range impacts and seek to ensure that the component parts of the business work together in a pro-active, flexible and responsive way.

In this chapter:
- Structural change in the international hospitality industry (A: 12 pp 204-212; A: 13 pp 221; E: 2 pp 31-35)
- Structural change in the internal environment (B: 12 pp 48-51; C: 7 pp 150-153)
- Hyatt's approach to co-ordinating realignments (E: 19 pp 339-345)
- Interfunctional dependency (A: 9 pp 145-147; F: 4 pp 49-73 & H: 5 pp 92-105)
- Structure, strategy and market co-alignment (E: 12 pp 199-220 & H: 6 pp 106-141)

REVIEW

Structural change in the international hospitality industry (A: 12 pp 204-212; A: 13 pp 221; E: 2 pp 31-35)
As noted in chapter 12, environmental changes continually influence the way in which firms organize their resources and interact with the marketplace. For example, in response to structural changes in supply and demand during the early 1990s, international hotel companies have had to monitor:
- the emergence of new international firms, partly as a consequent of acquisition and merger activity and the increasing influence of Pacific Rim developers;
- intense product development and branding activity;
- the scramble for prime site locations throughout Europe;
- the complex web of franchise, contract, joint venture and strategic alliance agreements used to off-set the rising costs and financial risks associated with development.

These are significant factors affecting the structure of the industry but they are by no means the only issues that hospitality/tourism firms must address if they are to maintain a balance between environmental change and organizational strategies and structure.

The global significance of hospitality/tourism development merits long-range environmental scanning activity so that the potential impact of complex environmental issues can be monitored and assessed over a period of ten years or more. In some instances, trends are reasonably well-documented and easy-to-interpret; current examples which might be categorized in this way include:
- *The asset evolution phenomenon.* Asset ownership tends to reflect economic prosperity; key changes are affecting: (a) Japan (long-term asset appreciation and concentration); (b) Europe (asset accumulation, but more difficult to achieve an adequate return on investment); (c) the USA (asset liquidation, growth in management contracts) and (d) the Asia-Pacific region (asset acquisition).
- *The technological flood.* Innovation in systems design, processing capability and connectivity is likely to revolutionize hotel guest room technology inputs, management decision support systems, global sales and marketing networks and transportation systems during this decade. Although the full potential of advanced technologies may not be fully utilized at present, hospitality/tourism firms could nevertheless evolve a ten year plan for harnessing the benefits of technological advances.
- *Product branding and segmentation.* The proliferation of brands aligned with different brand strategies is currently fuelled by the need to explore new markets and niche markets, fully exploit existing markets and above all, differentiate a given product-service configuration from rival offerings with similar

features at similar prices. Although activity is intense, successful formulas are comparatively easy to emulate.
- *Labour markets.* In the current and foreseeable economic climate, critical supply shortages are unlikely to occur, but many international firms are still seeking the 'ideal' organizational and cultural structure for managing a multinational, multicultural workforce and, at the same time, achieving incremental improvements in quality, productivity and profitability.

A number of more volatile trends will significantly affect hospitality/tourism development in the 1990s. These include:
- *Changing political systems.* It would seem likely that industrialists will continue to retain influence and power in capitalist countries, especially wherever political policies are largely non-interventionist. However, the position is much more confused in Eastern Europe, where politicians still exercise control of industry, despite the collapse of communism.
- *The green movement.* The pressing need for global conservation conflicts with aspects of current industry practice. The relationships between consumption of energy and other resources and waste (water, fuel, solids) are open to criticism and the global situation can only worsen as the pace of development increases.
- *Global wild cards.* There are many unpredictable factors affecting the pace and nature of change in the external environment. These include uncertain prospects for Eastern Bloc countries, the impact of newly industrialized nations on international markets, government regulation to control industry capacity and levels of pollution, trade and foreign investment policies and the financial security of major multinational companies.

Structural change in the internal environment (B: 12 pp 48-51; C: 7 pp 150-153)
As noted above, external forces are likely to compel hospitality/tourism firms to review and re-think their structures throughout the 1990s. Typically, the larger more bureaucratic-type organizations may find it harder to adapt to the accelerating rate of political, economic and social change. To compete effectively, firms will have to find ways of responding more quickly to customer tastes and expectations and, in making better use of advanced technology, the skills and knowledge base of employees will need to reflect this. Structural changes are likely to include:
- Flatter organizational structures with fewer levels of management, improved responsiveness and information processing capability;
- Managers who co-ordinate expert operatives rather than control subordinates;
- The wider use of cross-functional teams so that organizations can co-ordinate a greater number of simultaneous activities in place of fewer, sequential activities. This will reduce product development time and facilitate a sharper focus on more complex problems requiring combined expert knowledge.
- More decentralized operations which promote involvement through responsibility, participation and commitment from a better educated workforce. Some activities are likely to remain centralized in order to make best use of costly resources and highly specialized knowledge.
- Changes in personnel policy and practice so as recognise more widely the contribution made by employees and in particular, the rarity value of specialist skills and expertise considered to be of fundamental importance to the organization's success.
- Improved processes and procedures for developing and communicating strategy in response to sophisticated, fast-changing markets where a 'wait and see' approach is no longer effective.

Structural change in hospitality/tourism firms has greatly affected the range of tasks which operational managers now undertake:

"With head office staff reduced in number to the minimum possible and growth no longer the overriding strategy of most firms, unit managers are now being asked to perform differently. They are being asked to compete effectively on the local level, where conditions are becoming extremely competitive, to scan the environment for threats and opportunities, and to build a strategic plan for their units based on this type of analysis. This leaves the unit manager with the need to become a much more independent decision-maker and one who is much more aware of the forces in the environment and how they affect the future of the unit." M.D.Olsen (IJCHM, v3n4, 1991, p. 23.).

These and other forms of organizational change are likely to generate sources of tension and strain, especially if the structure and systems work against each other rather than together.

To prevent this happening, annual review questions might include: (a) what business are we in and how should we be competing? (b) what is the organization's main goal and the key success factors? (c) do departmental goals support or hinder the organization's goal? (d) are measures for evaluating departmental performance effective?

(e) do they help or prevent the department from contributing to the organization's goals? Further, annual reviews set in the context of evaluating overall strategic fit between the organization and environment help to provide an overview of many other important facets of the internal-external interface (see Figure 7.4, C: 7 p.151).

Hyatt's approach to co-ordinating realignments
(E: 19 pp 339-345)
Hyatt's strategic planning draws on one-year business plans, devised at regional and hotel level. This provides a flexible basis for making adjustments in line with external changes throughout the global hotel network. Realignment is facilitated by:

- The involvement of all managers from all departments in the cross-examination of local and regional trading conditions and the formulation of assumptions about events which are likely to affect general business environments in the near future.
- A review of plans and assumptions that have been made on a region-by-region basis by corporate staff at head office in Chicago in order to see how politics and economics have been interpreted.
- The formulation of a strategic overview of key global trends in the Americas, Europe and Asia-Pacific to provide the regions and individual hotels with a macro perspective to guide the preparation of detailed action plans.
- A stable, decentralized organization that facilitates rapid information transfer and encourages the development of both formal and informal networks between operational managers and functional specialists.
- Regular conferences and other events for managers to encourage the interchange of ideas, cultural perspectives and practices.
- A sustained emphasis on the importance of responsiveness to change, assisted by a comparatively flat corporate hierarchy, by giving greater autonomy to the regions and by encouraging managers to be entrepreneurial in planning, implementing and controlling hotel guest services.

Interfunctional dependency (A: 9 pp 145-147; F: 4 pp 49-73 & H: 5 pp 92-105)
By reviewing the organization and its component parts, it should be possible to identify sources of conflict which can cause a drift towards misalignment of systems, structure and environment. McKenna (1) comments on the importance of interfunctional dependency in organizations by describing inadequate linkages as 'broken chains'. Lee Iacocca encountered this problem when he began as chief executive at the American car giant Chrysler:

"The manufacturing guys would build cars without even checking with the sales guys. They just built them, stuck them in a yard, and then hoped that somebody would take them out of there. We ended up with a huge inventory and a financial nightmare." (2).

Internal systems and procedures should encourage integration between departments by establishing an internal market with relationships based on the external market model of customers and clients for each and every interaction and transaction.

Structure, strategy and market co-alignment
(E: 12 pp 199-220; E: 13 pp 221-227 & H: 6 pp 106-141)
In adapting organizational structure and strategy to changes in the marketplace, an opportunity exists to improve the fit between customer segments and the firm's product portfolio. The options for co-alignment can be viewed in terms of a matrix depicting the relationships between levels of market uncertainty and the fit with two generic service strategies; standardization and customization (see Figure 12.1; E: 12 p.207). In reality, the scope for changing from one to the other service strategy is mainly determined by the characteristics of the product, service design and delivery and organizational flexibility. The standardization approach underlies the successful trans-continental transfer of fast-food concepts, but customization is less well-established. Hilton International, among others, are developing customized service brands designed to achieve a precise fit with the expressed needs of specific market segments. For example, the importance of the Japanese outbound travel market prompted the design of a customized service package with a specific, albeit subtle appeal which helps to secure Japanese business without over-emphasizing its importance or alienating guests from other countries. In summary, there are five key design considerations for achieving product and market alignment (3):

- Wherever feasible, hospitality services should be customized by purpose of visit and/or origin of guest.

- Product consistency is essential to the retention of customer loyalty, especially during an expansion phase.

- Organizational flexibility and responsiveness to guest needs are essential to service development, especially in meeting guest expectations of localized inputs and cultural influences.

- Service-based differentiation of products helps customers to make a more realistic and accurate assessment of quality and value.

- Improvements to service quality and product design should draw on the full human resource capability of the organization.

CONCLUSION

The gathering pace of change in hospitality/tourism environments during the 1980s and 1990s means that alignment of structure and strategy has become an organizational imperative. Equally important is the need to maintain responsiveness to market trends by fostering interfunctional dependency, mechanisms for rapid information transfer and planning systems that allow sufficient flexibility at regional, divisional and unit levels for managers to interpret localized conditions and react accordingly. In this way the co-alignment with external markets is natural and organic rather than over-planned and insensitive to subtle yet often significant events.

Review questions:

1. Identify and assess the significance of long-range global trends which in your view, are likely to affect (a) the further expansion of fast-food chains and (b) the prospects for tourism development.

2. In view of the structural changes occurring inside hospitality/tourism firms, review the implications for managers working in operational and specialist roles.

3. Analyze and critically evaluate the methods used to maintain alignment between the structure, strategies and market segments served by a firm with which you are familiar.

References:

1. R.McKenna. *The Regis Touch.* Addison-Wesley, New York, 1985.
2. L.Iacocca with W.Novak. *Iacocca: An Autobiography.* Bantam Books, New York, 1984 p.162.
3. R.Teare. 'Designing a Contemporary Hotel Service Culture' *International Journal of Service Industry Management,* 4(2): 63-73, 1993.

EXTENSION

Read: Chapters 4 and 5 of *Achieving Quality Performance: Lessons from British Industry* (G)

Chapter 4 highlights the re-alignment of business strategy at ICL, a company on the verge of bankruptcy during the early 1980s.

Chapter 5 explains how Land Rover (LR) re-gained its market position and repuation by re-designing its processes and procedures to meet customer needs.

Extension questions: (chapter 4)

1. Evaluate the relative effectiveness of cost-cutting and marketing as strategies for improving productivity at ICL.

2. Identify how and why the quality management structure proposed by Crosby has been modified by ICL.

Practical exercises:

1. To what extent might the ICL quality management infrastructure assist an eqivalent sized hospitality firm to maintain internal-external alignment?

2. Identify the quality issues implied in the mission and strategies of a firm with which you are familiar. How might they be emphasized so as to promote interfunctional behaviour?

Extension questions: (chapter 5)

1. Evaluate the fit between LR's quality, efficiency and productivity goals. Has total quality improvement (TQI) made a difference?

2. Review the changes which occurred at LR and comment on the factors contributing to the eventual success of the TQI programme.

Practical exercises:

1. To what extent is LR's TQI methodology applicable to hospitality/tourism firms? Explain how necessary modifications might be addressed with reference to an example firm.

2. Assume your example firm has decided to use the TQI methodology. What internal changes and supportive measures would be needed to make it work?

15 SUSTAINING STRATEGIC FOCUS

INTRODUCTION

"Regardless of how large and sophisticated a hospitality company becomes, attention to detail in each individual establishment requires management in perpetuity. To facilitate progress and support change, it is necessary to keep under constant review the effectiveness of organizational structures, the flow of ideas and information, and the impact of training on employees and the business." R.Forte (A: 1 p.6.)

Continual, incremental or stepwise improvement in systems, processes and procedures has become a characteristic feature of successful organizations. It requires an ability to sustain an on-going quality improvement effort and, at the same time maintain the business focus needed to achieve consistency of performance across the organization. To harness the true potential for improvement, hospitality/tourism firms are increasingly embracing a total quality management philosophy. This provides a powerful catalyst for change by empowering employees to share responsibility for quality improvement and thereby the momentum needed to sustain unity of purpose and effort.

In this chapter:
- Total quality management: A philosophy for the 1990s? (B: 50 pp 205-208; E: 18 pp 326-338)
- Quality improvement philosophies and techniques (B: 46 & 47 pp 189-196)
- Increasing employee involvement (B: 4 pp 15-18; B: 48 pp 197-201)
- The role of recognition and reward systems (C: 2 pp 32-33)
- The role of quality circles in process improvement (B: 41 pp 170-173)
- TQM at Scott's Hotels Limited (E: 18 pp 327-338)

REVIEW

Total quality management: A philosophy for the 1990s? (B: 50 pp 205-208; E: 18 pp 326-338)
Management theories and styles tend to reflect evolving business environments, the nature and source of competitive threats and the changing dynamics of organizational life. It is possible to identify trends in business thinking and practice over the course of several decades; from the emergence of centralized planning, well suited to the comparatively stable economic and political environments of the 1950s, to the wider application of scientific management and production techniques in the 1980s. Quality is, and will most likely continue to be, the pre-eminent concern of manufacturing and service businesses in the 1990s. To achieve progress in process improvement, a total quality system is needed.

Oakland (1) defines total quality management (TQM) as an approach to improving the effectiveness and flexibility of businesses as a whole. It encompasses a way of organizing relationships so that every component part of the firm and every member of the workforce is encouraged to participate in the on-going processes of improving and developing the organization's business activities so as to meet the aspirations of stakeholders and fulfil the strategic mission. It represents both a philosophy of business and a workable system for sustaining the organization's strategic focus, by:
- Recognizing customers and discovering their needs;
- Setting standards which are consistent with customer requirements within and outside the organization;
- Continually monitoring all facets of business activity, seeking ways of achieving stepwise improvement;
- Establishing systems for maintaining quality performance;
- Equipping people to achieve quality performance in the context of policy established by management and leadership by example from management;
- Empowering people at every level in the organization to actively participate in quality improvement.

TQM requires the extension of the customer concept to every part and organizational process, thereby providing multiple links in a quality-driven chain with each employee acting as a supplier to the next employee until the consumer, the final customer in the chain, is served and satisfied. The chain also extends backwards to the organization's suppliers and so time and attention must be devoted to specifying and explaining the need for assuring the quality of supplier inputs. To maintain the connections throughout the chain, total involvement is needed (people, systems, processes, procedures) otherwise the quality of output to the external customer may ultimately be impaired.

Although the concept of TQM is appealing because of the level of employee commitment it tends to generate, it is a difficult and complex concept to fully implement and sustain. To succeed, an appropriate infrastructure is needed, typically characterized by a series of sequential steps:
- First, it requires considerable effort on the part of senior management who must find ways of generating enthusiasm for a radically different way of thinking and working. Initially, this requires a realignment of thinking brought about by selling the concept to the workforce, but it also requires leadership by example to demonstrate sincerity of purpose and to establish new norms of behaviour and working practices.
- Second, it requires a cultural change to bring quality to the forefront of organizational life and to reinforce intolerance of errors and defects.
- Third, the organization must establish an effective quality system with proven auditing procedures to support the focus on quality. In practice, a valuable step in this direction is to seek BS 5750 accreditation (see chapter 8).
- To implement and sustain TQM, the organization needs to set-up a network of quality teams to drive the quality improvement effort. This step often requires experimentation in order to find the best way of stimulating team effort within and across operational departments and specialist functions. To equip the teams for action, the organization needs to implant the necessary tools and techniques for problem identification and resolution and for monitoring the quality improvement effort.

Quality improvement philosophies and techniques (B: 46 & 47 pp 189-196)
A number of management philosophers and production techniques have influenced the development of total quality management systems:
- *W.Edwards Deming* popularized the view that management's role should be to set up and continuously improve the systems within which people work. This requires a collaborative effort as its success depends on feedback from those who actually do the job. To obtain this, employees need to be trained in the use of methods of work analysis and statistical process control and in this way, they become aware of where and how changes should be made.
- *Joseph M. Juran* argued that managers should adopt a broader approach to quality improvement by analyzing the systems in use as well as the quality of work and output of operatives. To identify improvement priorities, management should place all the main quality problems in rank order, decide which few improvements would yield the best results and set up projects to resolve them.
- *Just-in-time production* (JIT) - is closer to a business philosophy than a production technique because the underlying concept of producing goods only when they are needed, affects marketing and distribution as well as the production orientation. In reducing production batch sizes to a minimum, a number of benefits accrue. These include: (a) fewer, smaller quantity stock movements; (b) easier detection of quality problems; (c) easier detection of delays, errors and bottlenecks; (d) closer involvement of operatives in production control.
- *Total quality control* (TQC) - an approach based on collective responsibility for quality. It involves all employees in every department, thereby replacing the quality control function.
- *Zero defects* - a production/service ideal is the elimination of all sources of error. A positive way of pursuing this objective is to seek progressive process improvement rather than relying on inspection and detection to hold down the number of errors occurring. As with TQC, this approach requires a shift from specialists continually checking to operatives seeking ways of improving every activity and process from design to distribution and sales.

Increasing employee involvement (B: 4 pp 15-18; B: 48 pp 197-201)
In seeking a wider commitment to task and process improvement, it is essential to promote the value of the individual, regardless of their position and status in the organization. This is often undermined by a rather restricted view of organizational relationships whereby managers make decisions and subordinates carry them out. This both inhibits the creative potential of employees and negates the nature of the contribution they could make. To create the conditions for improving employee job satisfaction and with it a stronger sense of commitment to the tasks involved, it is necessary to ensure that every job is: (a) meaningful; (b) allows the individual to take some measure of responsibility for their efforts and results; (c) enables the individual to see an end result and obtain feedback on how well or badly they and the group or department they belong to is doing. In applying these criteria to assess the intrinsic value of each and every organizational role, it may be necessary to seek ways of enriching jobs by:
- *expanding the role horizontally,* to encompass activities previously undertaken prior to, or immediately after a particular process stage;
- *expanding the role vertically,* by devolving responsibility for planning and controlling work to the individual or group of people who undertake the work.

Individual aspirations, needs and abilities differ, but the psychological benefits of allowing employees to feel that they have some control over their work and in so doing, scope for solving problems and process improvement, are considerable. In highly controlled environments, the symptoms of employee frustration are often manifest in high absenteeism, low morale and poor productivity; attempts to gain greater commitment to the organization and its goals are therefore unlikely to succeed.

The role of recognition and reward systems
(C: 2 pp 32-33)
The closer the fit between objectives, employee needs and values and the mechanisms used to recognize and reward individual and team performance, the easier it becomes to maintain high levels of morale, motivation and productivity. Reward systems operate on two levels; the nature of the work itself can provide in-built or intrinsic reward if it is linked to realistic performance targets and if sufficient scope exists for the individual to contribute to the design and/or implementation of their work. Extrinsic reward in the form of pay, bonuses and benefits should constitute a fair, equitable and flexible structure, thereby encouraging employee confidence in the system and mutual trust between employees and management. The relationships between behaviour, performance and reward are often difficult to manage, especially if work groups or teams are encouraged to innovate or solve problems. This could for instance, lead to the formation of peer group behavioural norms which conflict with organizational rules and codes of behaviour.

The role of quality circles in process improvement
(B: 41 pp 170-173)
A quality circle normally consists of a group of employees who meet together regularly with a facilitator (usually but not always a supervisor or manager) to discuss, analyze and seek solutions to work-related issues. The formation of a quality circle structure generally signifies that an organization is: (a) committed to a desire to raise its performance by making small, incremental improvements and that (b) those closest to the day to day operating problems are best placed to try to identify and implement solutions. It also implies that senior management agree on two key considerations:
- A significant number of operational improvements could be made by the employees themselves without specific direction and guidance from managers;
- A willingness to accept an irreversible change in organizational dynamics by transferring some of the power and authority traditionally held by managers to the groups of employees running quality circles.

To ensure that quality circles work effectively, a number of conditions apply. These include: (a) a commitment from employees and a willingness to trust on the part of management; (b) the existence of genuine operating problems to solve; (c) a willingness by management to accept the consequences of eliciting employees' opinions and to act on reasonable proposals made by the circles; (d) acceptance of the need for circle training to include topics such as problem-solving, creative thinking, participating in meetings, communicating and giving presentations; (e) a need to recognize and reward achievement; (f) periodic reinforcement by management of the importance and value of the quality circle structure to the process of quality improvement. Typically, a properly functioning quality circle structure will generate:
- improvements in productivity, safety, production and service delivery, morale and communications;
- a greater awareness interfunctional dependency (see chapter 14);
- ownership of quality issues pertaining to the operational roles of the circle members;
- improvements to the work environment, making it easier to introduce change.

TQM at Scott's Hotels Limited (E: 18 pp 327-338)
The implementation of TQM at Scott's Hotels is underpinned by evolving structures and processes which above all, lay emphasis on quality improvement through teamworking at every level in the organization. Incremental progress can be viewed in terms of two stages; establishing the foundations (1989-91) and second, consolidating and building (1992-93) (see J.Hubrecht et al, IJCHM, v5n3, 1993, pp i-viii).

The move towards TQM began in 1989 with the launch of a quality circles programme and the appointment of a quality support manager (QSM). The QSM provided a link between the managing director's TQM leadership and co-ordination for the rapidly expanding quality circle activity at unit level. To support circle team development, a training programme was implemented in 1990/91. This included sessions on communication and relationship building, team dynamics and problem-solving tools and techniques. The company's own *Quality Guide for Fortune Seekers* TQM training programme was also launched during this period.
Scott's partnership with Marriott, which began in January 1992, has had a number of synergistic benefits, notably in relation to TQM. Scott's now use a three phase TQM programme covering:

(a) employee empowerment; (b) problem solving and communication and (c) advance problem solving and leadership skills to support the circles and two new structures; quality improvement teams and hotel action teams.

Summarizing, Scott's TQM programme plays a central role in sustaining strategic focus. Key priorities which form an integral part of the total organizational effort include: (a) improving customer retention; (b) reducing staff turnover and (c) improving profitability. Collectively, these issues provide a challenge which every employee is invited to share. Jan Hubrecht, Scott's managing director, explains:

"Employees now have much more involvement in operations and they have developed further the ability to respond to guest feedback in a positive way. There is also a stronger sense of striving for excellence in the individual hotels arising from the unity of purpose and greater team involvement. This in turn has led to a better understanding and awareness of the key factors affecting the business as a whole, at every level in the organization."

CONCLUSION

Ultimately, consistent performance regardless of the trading conditions is the hallmark of a well run business. TQM provides a means of fully utilizing the potential that exists inside hospitality/tourism firms through the active participation of people - its most valuable resource.

Review questions:

1. To what extent do you agree with the proposition that TQM is a suitable business philosophy for the 1990s?

2. Identify the barriers to achieving wider employee involvement in the task of maintaining strategic focus. Support your analysis with reference to specific examples.

3. Outline your recommendations for setting up and supporting a quality circles programme in a firm of your choice. Choose a firm which currently lacks a quality management policy.

References:

1. J.S.Oakland. *Total Quality Management.* Heinemann, Oxford, 1989.

EXTENSION

Read: Chapters 1 and 3 of *Achieving Quality Performance: Lessons from British Industry* (G)

Chapter 1 focuses on Amersham International's (AI) efforts to sustain a successful quality improvement programme and stimulate wider participation.

Chapter 3 describes how Hydrapower Dynamics (HD) have sought to extend the TQM concept by becoming a learning-centred organization.

Extension questions: (chapter 1)

1. Evaluate the effectiveness of AI's four phase quality improvement approach in terms of its ability to sustain strategic direction and focus.

2. How might AI's quality improvement programme benefit from lessons learned?

Practical exercises:

1. Relate AI's phase 3 (increased participation) to a hospitality/tourism firm with which you are familiar. What improvements are feasible?

2. Devise a framework for evaluating structure and strategy co-alignment in a hospitality/tourism firm. Comment on the evaluative tests you would use and how they might be applied.

Extension questions: (chapter 3)

1. To what extend is BS5750 accreditation helpful in assisting small firms to become fully committed to TQM? What problems might they encounter?

2. What in your view, are the characteristic features of a 'learning organization'. How has HD benefited from its capacity to learn and improve?

Practical exercises:

1. Examine the concepts of external awareness, manoeuvrability and change potential in two organizations (large and small) of your choice. Comment on the differences of approach.

2. Evaluate the nature of the contact each of the two organizations has with its customers. Comment on the measures used to listen to customers and maintain a sense of closeness.